Interviews with Indie Authors

Top Tips from Successful Self-Published Authors

Interviews with Indie Authors
Copyright © 2012 Claire Ridgway and Tim Ridgway

ISBN-13: 978-1478295914
ISBN-10: 1478295910

All rights reserved. No part of this publication may be reproduced, stored in a retrieval system, or transmitted, in any form or by any means, electronic, mechanical, photocopying, recording or otherwise, except as permitted by the UK Copyright, Designs and Patents Act 1988, without the prior permission of the publisher.

For more information on
MadeGlobal Publishing, visit our website:
www.madeglobal.com

Contents

Michael 'madbot' McCloskey .. 5
Nick Russell 15
Connie Suttle 19
Michael Prescott 25
Terri Reid 33
Hugh Howey 39
Scott Nicholson 45
Kristen Ashley 49
Aaron Patterson 55
Carol Luce Davis 59
Claire Ridgway 65
Alexa Grace 71
Marie Force 77
Shadonna Richards 83
Colleen Hoover 87
Barbara Freethy 93
Joseph Lallo 97

Rebecca Forster 103
Caryn Moya Block 107
Denise Grover Swank 111
Mainak Dhar 119
Imogen Rose 125
CJ Lyons 129
Bella Andre 133
Theresa Ragan 137
Maria Murnane 143
Russell Blake 147
Linda Welch 153
Debra Holland 161
J. Thorn 167
James Somers 173
Karen Cantwell 177
Tracey Garvis Graves 183
Elena Greene 189

Foreword

The world of publishing has changed beyond recognition over the past few years, and this change has created a new interest in the written word by readers and writers alike.

My first memory of self-publishing was with my Grandfather creating a book of his memories of being the Chaplain at Stalag Luft III camp when the "Great Escape" happened. This book was painstakingly hand typed and manually laid out in book format. It was bulk printed by what we would today call a "vanity" publisher because it didn't have mass market appeal. A great book was created ... and then it sat in storage boxes for many many years. Such a shame, and something that doesn't need to happen today.

Fast forward twenty years and things are very different. With the advent of true "print on demand" services from companies like CreateSpace and Lulu, and with computers, word processors and desktop publishers wildly available, it is now within reach of everyone to have their book in print for next to no cost. And of course with the growing trend for people to own e-readers, it is even easier for a book to be produced and sold.

Since the birth of Internet as we know it in 1992, the world has changed dramatically. We are truly in the "information age", where what you know is more important that what you can do. This change has created some casualties as you'll see through this book. For one thing, the traditional bookshop is being squeezed out of the market, replaced by virtual online bookshops. For another, the role of literary agents and the the traditional publisher have dramatically changed, though some may not have fully seen how much of a change there has been. I make no judgement on whether this is a good or a bad thing ... but self-publishing is most definitely a good thing for today's authors.

So, armed with just a computer, you too can bring your book to life. And if you are anything like the writers within this book, you'll soon be making an exceptional number of sales. There has never been a time like the present for getting your work "out there", and I encourage you to start now.

To your amazing success,

Tim Ridgway

A note about this book and charity....

We believe in giving back to charity as a way to improve the lives of others around the world. In particular, we feel that the people of Africa are in great need of help. Because of this we have decided to give half of the profits from sales of this book to great causes in Africa.

Thank you for your support of these charities through your purchase of this book!

Rope
(Relief for Oppressed
People Everywhere)

Goal for
The Gambia

Michael 'madbot' McCloskey

Introduction

Michael "madbot" McCloskey self-published his first novel, "Slave of Chu Kutall", back in 2005, but is best known for his Synchronicity Trilogy and Trilisk books.

The Interview

Tell us about yourself and your background?

I am a software engineer in Silicon Valley afflicted with recurring dreams of otherworldly creatures, mysterious alien planets and fantastic adventures.

What is your writing philosophy?

I write to please myself first. I would lose interest if it wasn't something I enjoyed myself, and I suspect my perfect set of readers would lose interest as well.

I stay away from Good vs. Evil boredom. It appears that books need conflict to keep interest, but that conflict is all too often a struggle between Good and Evil. Good and Evil are made up in our minds and defined differently by everyone anyway. But it's more than that: When you read such a book what side is going to win in the end? Good. When the protagonist gets into a big fight with Evil

GENRE
Science Fiction

in the middle of the book, is he/she going to die? No. When the book opens does it look like Good is doomed? Yes. B-O-R-I-N-G.

In my books, there are different forces in conflict. They are not really Good and Evil. It may not be at all clear who you are supposed to "root for". The various characters probably all have what you consider to be both admirable qualities and flaws. You may not know what side is going to win. I find that more interesting and I hope you do, too.

> **Doing things in person, such as book signings, simply does not scale. This new industry is a global market.**

I like to create uncertainty in the outcome. When you watch a TV show, when the good guy detective gets into a tight spot, are you sitting there sweating it out wondering if they are about to die? Nope. They can't die. And when at the end of the episode, if there was an explosion and it looks like they died, are you afraid they did? No. Imagine if you knew the detective only had a random number of episodes to live. Each time they broke into that apartment to find clues, you'd have to wonder: are they about to get shot dead? Why, you'd actually have to watch the show and see what happens.

Major characters can meet their doom in the middle of my books. You have to read it to find out who lives and who dies. In my opinion, this is more entertaining than the cliché, recycled stuff we get day in and day out where you already know what is going to happen, even at the cost of risking the investment the reader has made in the character, because that investment is worth less if they know exactly what's going to happen.

What made you decide to self-publish?

I wanted to pursue a lifelong dream of being an author. The e-book revolution empowered me to do exactly that. Make no mistake, the barriers to self-publishing are very low, and it's a very rewarding endeavor even if you don't sell a huge number of books.

How long have you been self-publishing?

About five or six years.

What has been the most effective thing that you have done to promote your book?

Advertising on the internet. Doing things in person, such as book signings, simply does not scale. This new industry is a global market. I don't spend much time on things that don't scale to many customers. So, I advertise online with companies that can reach millions of potential customers in a targeted way, like Google, Facebook, Goodreads, etc.

Do you do anything that you consider out of the ordinary to make your book a success?

I don't think it should be out of the ordinary, but... from what I hear from customer complaints, many indie authors don't use professional editors. And from what I see, many indie authors don't work with professional illustrators. I assume both of these are due to monetary restrictions.

> **One thing that surprised me here is that strong sales in one genre transfer few sales to other genres by the same author.**

I look at these books as an investment (of time and money). I don't expect to make money on the first few books. I hope to make money much later after building a name for myself and offering many books. And the bottom line is, I will do this whether or not I make any money because I love doing it.

My web pages offer many different choices for sources of reviews and vendors. I refuse to lock myself into just one vendor.

Online advertising does not seem economically viable. You have found otherwise?

It reminds me of the Drake Equation. It can go absolutely nowhere fast if the conversion percentages in each link in the chain are too low. If your offering has that X factor across the board, from display image, to blurb, to sample, to price, to you have authored lots of books, then you can sell enough to pay for your advertising. Otherwise, it is a loss.

There is some number of people who go to look at your book. You increase that number with an investment in advertising.

Some percent of that number will click on an image depending on its appeal to your audience. You maximize that fraction with a captivating image. Some fraction of the people who like the image will read your blurb. You maximize the number of people who will read your sample by making the blurb hook them hard. Then based on your first chapter some fraction will buy also based on your price. Then, some fraction of people like your book and go looking for another one written by you without having to be netted by your advertising again. Some fraction of them will mention you to their friends. You can't get to the valuable end part of this chain without some investment in time and money. There is no guarantee the investment will work unless you have good fractions all the way down the chain.

If you stick with it for years and build up a selection of books, and a base of fans, then of course it gets easier. That is my goal now. I have no idea how much success I will ultimately see, but I'm committed to it because I love to write novels.

You measure as much of each of these steps as you can to find weak factors in your equation.

Just for yuks here is a hypothetical walk-through:

~33,000,000 impressions a month x .14% click through = ~47,000 clicks x 5% read sample = ~2400 samples read x 40% acquisition rate = ~950 copies sold. 70 of these mention the book to their friends. 50 of these become fans and buy more work by the author. 10 of them mention it on their blogs and social accounts.

Two shortcuts through this miasma exist: if you have invested enough to get up on the sales charts, then you get what is essentially free advertising, as people browsing sales websites see your stuff on bestseller lists. If your buyers like your book then you get more free advertising by "word of mouth" (which includes blogs, posts, etc these days).

These secondary effects (for instance being at the top of the High Tech Science Fiction ladder at Amazon) may increase those sales driven by your advertising by an order of magnitude. But that requires an investment which may pay off or may have been wasted, depending on what all your factors work out to be.

Another bit of good news is that as you advertise, your efficiency increases if you're paying attention and nudging things in the right direction. At first, your cost per click may be high. Your click through rate may initially be low. Many people give up at this point. However, I learned that as the system adapts and finds areas where it gets clicks, the cost per click went down for me. Eventually it was very cheap per click. At first I was quite happy with this and it was helping. But then I discovered the next stage. In the endgame, you're not actually seeking the lowest cost clicks out there: they may be useless clicks. You need to track your conversions and pay more for the good clicks: ones from sites more likely to deliver people who are actually interested in your product.

As an example of useless clicks, let me tell you an experience of mine. I have a tablet device at home. My three year old enjoys using it. The free kid's games and learning programs sometimes come with ads(!) in them. When my three year old clicks on an ad for a lawn mower, that is a bad click. Its cost was probably low, but it doesn't matter. It was a waste. If you track conversions, then you will know the ads coming from places like that are worthless and you won't pay much, if anything for them.

It takes time for an online ads system to identify where good clicks are coming from and it takes a while to set up your conversion data to feed into the system. So once again, this is an investment: you are losing money at first in hopes of getting money later. It comes with no guarantees. But it is up to you and your hard work to determine the outcome. Advertising is a skill just like writing books. I'm a bit odd in that I actually find advertising to be a fun challenge: it's just another puzzle to figure out. Besides, I can't write for more than three or four hours in any given day. My creativity just dries up.

I have gained some experience with this, but I cannot predict the outcome until I try each book. Some of them have good responses and some don't. Maybe I'll become good at predicting them, but right now I'm not.

If someone doesn't have any money to use for this, then I suggest you simply keep writing good books and accumulate a small library first. Then, any success you have will be multiplied by the fact that fans can find a lot more of your work to go buy. Then you can start advertising later when you have more to gain from each fan you make. The number of books in your name are a resource you can grow for free and they multiply any investment you make later. I think making any profit on just one book is very difficult (of course, exceptions exist and more are coming).

How have you gone about getting the word out about your book?

I work with companies that mass advertise in very targeted ways (no spamming). Modern advertising is about reaching people you know are likely to be interested. It's not like the old school methods such as running an ad in a newspaper where only one in ten thousand would care about your product if they even noticed it.

What has been your most successful self-published book, and how many have you sold ?

Trilisk Ruins. I've sold about 16K in four months. Its sales have driven more sales in my other science fiction novels. One thing that surprised me here is that strong sales in one genre transfer few sales to other genres by the same author.

What are your top tips for new indie authors?

Obviously it starts with your product. So work hard, but on projects that please yourself, not some other imagined audience. Develop your skill using online writing workshops. Grow a thick skin. You have to listen to criticism and consider it, but in the end, you are the one who has to decide if it is valid.

When it comes to publishing, work with professional editors and illustrators. Construct a nice website. Advertise using the internet in ways that scale to millions of people.

What do you think about the future of the publishing world?

The future is already here! ;-) In this new age of electronic publishing, the barriers have been removed from publishing your own books. It no longer takes money up front to publish like it used to. And so the old publishing houses are in trouble. They used to take the risk of publishing someone they thought was good, by paying the up front cost of printing, distributing, and advertising the books, in exchange for a big cut of the profit. So they screened out authors they didn't think would sell.

People still ask me: Have you got a publisher? An agent? It makes me laugh. I feel satisfaction knowing all those old world publishers are slowly languishing in their own little bubble, thinking they still have a place in the new world of electronic publishing, thinking that people still need to come to them to publish a book, that they still have control, with the authors hiring agents and groveling at their feet for the chance to get a book looked at. It took most of them a decade to even decide to accept email submissions! I hope they wake up when it's far too late for them to do anything, and they realize all their years of arrogance and formula-book publishing has come back to bite them.

Today, if a traditional publisher offers you a contract, I hope you respond "Sorry, I don't accept simultaneous submissions" and refer them to your Publication Offer Guidelines page. Because it no longer takes money up front to publish. For now, the middleman is cut down to size. Enjoy it while it lasts, it's only a matter of time before the middleman works back into the equation.

I focus on e-books, because dead tree scrolls are a thing of the past. Humans give up their traditions reluctantly. You can drag your feet or you can participate in the future.

Any other thoughts you would like to share?

I'd like to mention the importance of reviews in the new industry. It is now mostly reader's reviews that serve to screen the books (not just on sales sites like Amazon, but also on reader community sites like Goodreads). The publishing houses used to screen out "bad" books (often that meant books that did not fit a formula). Now, with electronic books, a potential buyer has the author name, the blurb, the sample, and some reviews to look at in order to make a buying decision. So please review books, or at least rate them. If you like them, tell the potential buyer, and if you didn't like one, warn the buyer away. This will help the new system work in the absence of big publisher screening. I for one don't want to go back to the old system! I think having just a few publishing editors deciding what "flavor" of books should be out there stifled the diversity we had. Most of the books out there were from formulas the publishers had success with before. B-O-R-I-N-G. Well, at least after you have read a few dozen books about the same kind of good guys in the same impossible situations that manage to win anyway in super predictable fashion...

Author Websites

http://www.squidlord.com/home/writings
http://www.facebook.com/madbotmccloskey

Link to the Author's Amazon Author page

http://www.amazon.com/Michael-McCloskey/e/B005WBM686/

Nick Russell

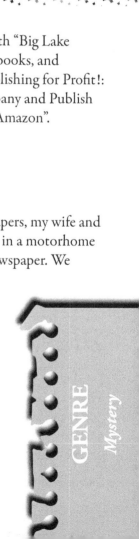

Introduction

Author Nick Russell's debut mystery novel, "Big Lake", has sold over 107,000 copies since he published it in January 2012 and he quickly followed it with "Big Lake Lynching". Nick has also written RV and travel books, and co-written "The Step-by-Step Guide to Self-Publishing for Profit!: Start Your Own Home-Based Publishing Company and Publish Your Non-Fiction Book with CreateSpace and Amazon".

The Interview

Tell us about yourself and your background?

After a career publishing small town newspapers, my wife and I have spent the last 13+ years traveling fulltime in a motorhome and publishing the Gypsy Journal RV Travel Newspaper. We travel over 10,000 miles a year. So as I write, the view out my window may be the wild Oregon coast, or an Arizona mountain vista, or the deep green mountains of Kentucky.

What made you decide to self-publish?

I have no patience for the traditional publishing route, or for allowing some agent or editor to decide if my work is worthy. I approach publishing as a business, and the

GENRE *Mystery*

quickest and surest way to success in that business was to be my own boss and make my own decisions.

How long have you been self-publishing?

I have self-published RV, travel, and niche books and booklets for over 13 years. Before that, I owned small town newspapers in Washington, Oregon, and Arizona. Is that self-publishing too?

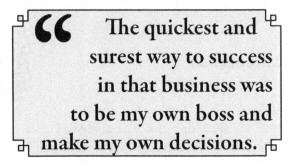

What has been the most effective thing that you have done to promote your book?

I have worked hard to build a large and loyal readership through my daily blogs, the Gypsy Journal, and social networking sites. So I had a built in audience before my Big Lake series was even published.

Do you do anything that you consider out of the ordinary to make your book a success?

Writing is the easy part, once your book has been published, the real work begins. I work at marketing every day. I hear authors tell me over and over that they hate marketing. But that's the only way you can sell books.

How have you gone about getting the word out about your book?

I write several blogs, I have a Facebook author page, my bio is on Amazon, I use Twitter, it all adds up. I also have a loyal following who mention my books in their tweets and Facebook posts. It's like dropping a pebble into a pond, the ripple effect reaches out much further than I ever could myself.

What has been your most successful self-published book, and how many have you sold?

My first mystery novel, Big Lake, has sold over 107,000 copies in its first twelve months, mostly in Amazon Kindle format. But it is also on Smashwords and in print format.

What are your top tips for new indie authors?

Write a good book. Not just a good story, but pay attention to spelling, grammar, and punctuation. I see so many books that could make it, but as a reader I get turned off by errors any school kid should be able to spot. Have somebody else proof and edit your book. I use at least 2 and sometimes 3 different proof readers for each book.

What do you think about the future of the publishing world?

We are in the early stages of a revolution. E-books and print on demand technology are making traditional publishing houses obsolete. I think we will see publishing, and publishing support (proof readers, editors, cover designers, etc.) become cottage industries. The playing field has been leveled and anybody can

Top Tips from Successful Self-Published Authors

become an author/publisher. We'll see a lot of absolute junk out there by those who are not willing to make the effort to produce good work, bur we'll also see some amazing success stories.

Any other thoughts you would like to share?

Start today! Every day you are not writing, not publishing, not marketing are days and opportunities you will never have again.

Author Websites

http://gypsyjournalrv.com/category/nicksblog/
http://www.facebook.com/NickRussellAuthor

Link to the Author's Amazon Author page

http://www.amazon.com/Nick-Russell/e/B00520F10M/

Connie Suttle

Introduction

Fantasy novelist Connie Suttle is known for her popular Blood Destiny series and her YA series, Legend of the Ir'Indicti. She published ten books in just ten months and her fans are hungry for more. Connie will be publishing another four books in 2012!

The Interview

Tell us about yourself and your background

I've lived in Oklahoma all my life. During that time, I've done everything from mowing lawns to painting signs to teaching college courses. I have an MFA from the University of Oklahoma and have taught courses in Film Production, Animation and Film History. My most recent vocation (before I began writing seriously) was working as a manager for Borders. I left the company in 2007 and have been writing (seriously and furiously) ever since.

What made you decide to self-publish?

I sent out query letters for Blood Wager (Blood Destiny #1) in 2009. In total, I sent out six letters. For anyone who has done a query letter, you know you'll receive responses

GENRE: *Fantasy/ Science Fiction*

from some agents and absolute silence from others. I received a mixture of both. I know six queries isn't a lot, but the waiting (and rejection) was difficult, and came at a time when difficult wasn't an easy thing to deal with.

Anyone who has read my early blog posts knows that my husband almost died in 2007. He lay unconscious for weeks in a room in ICU while I was forced to handle everything, from struggling to pay bills and keeping everything else moving forward to worrying about what I might do if he didn't make it. I turned to writing, something I'd always planned to do but never really found the time for (except for the odd short story or partially-finished manuscript). I wrote while I sat at my husband's bedside. I wrote while I sat in waiting rooms later, during doctor visits or during dialysis treatments or any number of other things. Writing was therapy for me. Therefore, when I began sending out query letters and receiving rejections, I came to the decision that maybe waiting wasn't the best thing for me right then. After all, my husband and I had been presented with the stark reality that nobody is guaranteed the next day.

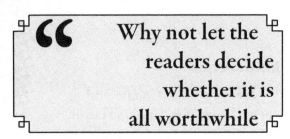
"Why not let the readers decide whether it is all worthwhile"

I stopped writing query letters for Blood Wager, but kept writing the series. At that point, I couldn't stop myself. Eventually, nine books were written in that series, followed by another six books for another series, and finally five more in the most recent series (Legend of the Ir'Indicti). I didn't send query letters again until I'd finished Bumble, the first in the Legend series. For that book, I sent out a total of twelve queries. Still not a lot by anyone's standards. I got two letters showing mild interest in Bumble, but not enough to gain an agent.

In 2011, after I'd written more than thirty books, I decided that the time had come. I either needed to send out more query letters (a lengthy and time-consuming enterprise) or I could take the plunge and publish my work as e-books. At that time, I never expected more than a handful of people to read my work, and most of those would be friends and family. I'd spent so much time and effort in creating the books, though, and basically thought, What the hell? I can pay for a cover image and get someone to help edit before publishing Blood Wager.

How long have you been self-publishing?

I published Blood Wager at the end of June, 2011.

What has been the most effective thing that you have done to promote your book?

That isn't an easy question to answer, because I feel it is a combination of things, rather than one or two things, that has helped in the long term. In the beginning, before I published, I set up a website and joined Facebook and Twitter. Everything I'd read before self-publishing my first book said I needed those things to gain contact with readers. At first I did a very inexpensive version of a website, but it was enough to put up images of my books

and give information on them, in addition to a short author bio. After publishing at the end of June, 2011, I gave away gift copies of Blood Wager. My friends and family helped, convincing many people to download free versions of e-readers to their phones or computers, just so they could give a free copy of my book a try.

I was also lucky enough to get two bloggers to do a review of the book, again through the efforts of a friend who was also looking to publish her book.

At one point, I emailed friends and family, offering to send gift copies of the book (up to ten copies each) to their friends or family, all I needed was for them to mention it to the recipients and get an email address for the e-book delivery. Yes, I had to set aside a budget for that, but honestly, I gave away less than a hundred copies of Blood Wager - many of them went ahead and bought the book instead of receiving the gift copy. After all, I'd priced Blood Wager at $0.99, so not a lot of money was being spent to send gift copies or to purchase the book outright.

I also advertised on a few book blogs. These ads were inexpensive - often $25.00 to run an ad for an entire month. Again, this was fitted into the budget I'd set for myself. I never went overboard in advertising or giving copies away. That's when the strangest thing happened - people read the book, and they started telling their friends and family about it. I published Blood Passage (#2) September 1, 2011, and Blood Sense (#3) September 15, 2011. The reason I published these two so closely together is that Blood Passage ended on a cliffhanger, so I didn't want to leave any readers I might have hanging in suspense. It turned out to be a good move. After selling perhaps 200 copies of Blood Wager in July and August, sales began to rise in September. People were talking about my books and they began climbing the ranks on Amazon.

Do you do anything that you consider out of the ordinary to make your book a success?

The only thing that might be out of the ordinary is my

publishing schedule. I'd written 30 books before I self-published the first one. These books were already written, although some of them required more editing and revising than others. In the past ten months, I've published ten books. In that time, too, I've sold more than 100,000 books. No, I never thought that would happen - I just wanted to get my work to the public. I wasn't thinking about sales or fans or reviews at the time; I just remember staring at the multiple files of manuscripts on my computer and thinking that it was so much work—why not let the readers decide whether it was all worthwhile?

What has been your most successful self-published book, and how many have you sold?

Blood Wager is the most successful to date, and I've probably sold around 25,000. I keep telling myself I need to sit down and compile actual figures, but I'm too busy writing and editing at the moment.

What are your top tips for new indie authors?

Write the next book. And then write the next one after that.

What do you think about the future of the publishing world?

That is a good question, and one I'm not sure I'm qualified to answer. Besides, there are other, more experienced self-published authors who are tackling that question in interviews and on their blogs. The best answer I can give is that it will certainly be different. The old, standard way of book publishing has already been blown away, I just think that many haven't opened their eyes wide enough to see it. I read many blogs, written by self-published authors as well as the traditionally published. At times, the meeting of the two seems like tectonic plates, crashing into one another. Yes, it can be grating, bordering on the verbally violent. In a few years, however, we may have a single, publishing continent, with some lovely, high mountains resulting from the merger. That's my hope, anyway.

Author Websites

http://subtledemon.com/

Link to the Author's Amazon Author page

http://www.amazon.com/Connie-Suttle/e/B00596DWR8/

Michael Prescott

Introduction

Suspense novelist Michael Prescott was stunned when he sold 800,000 books in 2011, his first full year of being self-published, and he's glad that he took the step to publish his work, both new and his backlist. He is one of today's bestselling e-book authors and his books include the New York Times bestselling "Stealing Faces" and "Blind Pursuit".

The Interview

Tell us about yourself and your background.

I had a pretty long career in traditional publishing from the mid-1980s until around 2007. At that point I found it impossible to get published, because the mass-market paperback end of the book industry had contracted dramatically. Since the vast majority of popular fiction made its money in paperback, this meant there was less demand on the part of publishers for the kind of commercial fiction I write. Basically you had to get a hardcover deal, and since all the paperback writers were scrambling for a limited number of hardcover slots, the situation was very competitive.

What made it worse was that publishers were cutting back on their staffs, streamlining operations, and engaged in other cost-cutting measures, so that editors were very reluctant to acquire anything that wasn't seen as a sure-fire hit. Unless you had something that looked like the next Da Vinci Code, you were hard-pressed to make a sale.

After failing to sell two novels in a row, I figured my print career was pretty much over, and I started making money by trading stocks and stock options.

What made you decide to self-publish?

Originally, I got into self-publishing to release a book called Riptide, which had been rejected by 25 publishers. It seemed that the only way to ever get this book out there was to publish it myself. I didn't expect it to sell many copies. It was more of a vanity project. Essentially I wanted a copy for my shelf, and I also wanted the fun of designing the cover and the layout. The print edition was published as a print-on-demand title through CreateSpace, a division of Amazon.

At first I didn't plan on doing an e-book edition at all, but when I saw how easy it was to put out the book in Kindle format, I decided I might as well do it. The Kindle edition eventually sold far more copies than the print edition, but that wasn't what I expected at the time.

I released Riptide in the summer of 2010. A little later, I decided to start releasing some of my backlist titles. These books had already been published but had gone out of print, and the rights had reverted to me. I wanted to keep the books in circulation, since I'd put a lot of work into them. I still didn't expect to sell many copies because up to then Riptide hadn't made me much money.

I invested in a high-speed scanner, the Fujitsu ScanSnap S1500, and an optical character recognition program called ABBYY FinePrint. Though I didn't expect to make back my investment on the equipment and software in the near future, I thought that in a year or two I might break even. So you can see that my expectations were very modest.

But in the early summer of 2011, when I had a few titles in release as Kindle editions, things started to change very quickly.

Why did the situation change?

I have to give due credit to a friend and fellow author, J. Carson Black, who was also experimenting with self-publishing. She'd had success with pricing her e-books at only $0.99 and promoting them on Amazon's discussion boards. I was skeptical, because I was still thinking in terms of the print industry and the usual cost of a paperback book, which is $8 and up. But e-book buyers are much more price conscious and are not willing to pay paperback prices for most titles, especially self-published titles by authors they haven't heard of.

So after some hesitation I tried lowering my prices to $0.99

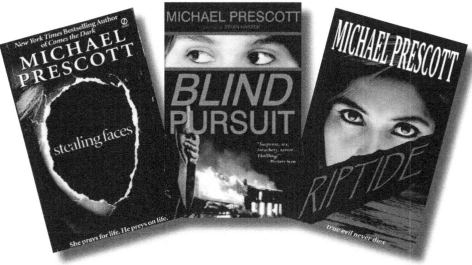

across-the-board, and I went on to the discussion boards at Amazon - particularly the boards that focused on bargain-priced books - and promoted my wares. And sales picked up dramatically. There was a real snowball effect from one month to the next. Before long, despite the lower prices, the books were generating far more money, simply because of the volume of sales.

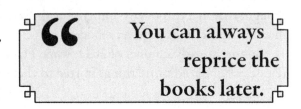

By the middle of the summer I could see that I was going to make more money from my e-books than from trading stocks. By the fall some of the titles had even hit mainstream bestseller lists like the New York Times and USA Today. Ultimately I sold about 800,000 books in 2011, and almost all those sales came in the second half of the year.

Do you do anything that you consider out of the ordinary to make your books successful?

I wouldn't call it out of the ordinary, but there are some things I'd recommend doing. First, price the book appropriately. I don't know if it's still necessary to debut the book at $0.99. The market changes quickly, and there are more e-book readers all the time, so you may be able to get away with a little higher price point. But I probably wouldn't go above $2.99 right now, and maybe lower if you're just getting started and want to build word-of-mouth. You can always reprice the books later, something I've done myself; all my titles are now $2.99 because I think the $0.99 price point has pretty much played itself out for me.

It's also a good idea to use the Amazon forums that I mentioned. But because Amazon has cracked down on authors promoting themselves, you have to restrict your self-promotional efforts to the Meet Our Authors section of the discussion boards.

Amazon encourages you to post links and advertising copy on those boards, but will react negatively if you start promoting yourself in other forums. It's not a good idea to do more than, say, five self-promotional comments in a day. Space them out over time so you're not flooding the boards.

Finally, you have to make sure that you're selling a good, attractive product. Take the time to put together a nice cover. I use an online service called Dreamstime that sells royalty-free images at reasonable prices. Usually I stitch together two or more images using Photoshop Elements, though any good photo-editing software should work. What you want is a colorful, arresting cover image that looks good as a thumbnail and also full-size.

Of course, the quality of the book itself is paramount, and this includes the readability of the text. In one case, I released a digital edition that had a lot of typos. I got some complaints, and I think it hurt sales. Since then I've been more careful about proofreading. It's not a bad idea to hire a freelance proofreader to check your work.

How have you gone about getting the word out about your book?

Besides the Amazon boards, I've found Facebook, email, and my author site to be the most effective tools.

What has been your most successful self-published book, and how many have you sold?

Believe it or not, I haven't kept close track of the individual titles. What interested me was the sales in aggregate, which have now surpassed one million copies. In general, I would say the ones that sold best were fast-paced, action-oriented books. Those that are a little more subtle and character-oriented have also sold well, but not quite as well.

In some ways, I think e-books are reviving the market for pulp fiction—fast, fairly short novels that can be read quickly as pure entertainment. Naturally there are many success stories in the e-book field, but it seems to me that a disproportionate number of them involve what might be called pulp, and I include my own books in that category. Mainstream publishers have perhaps underestimated the public appetite for books that are just fun to read, without necessarily being artistic breakthroughs or intellectual puzzles.

For instance, there used to be a huge market for "cozies" - drawing room mysteries of the Agatha Christie type–but today relatively few books like that are being published. I would guess there's still a good-sized audience out there for cozies, but they aren't being served by traditional publishers. That's another area where e-books might take up the slack.

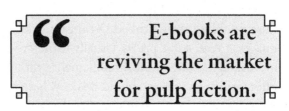

E-books are reviving the market for pulp fiction.

What do you think about the future of the publishing world?

I'm not quite as apocalyptic about it as some people are. I doubt that mainstream publishing is simply going to disappear. What I do think is that mass-market paperbacks will largely go away, replaced by digital books. Before too long you'll be able to buy a good quality e-book reading device at the supermarket for $25. It will be like buying a disposable camera. When you get to that point, nearly everyone who reads for pleasure will be reading e-books at least some of the time. The main virtues of mass-market paperbacks are that they're relatively cheap and portable, but e-books will be even cheaper and more portable, so I expect them to displace the smaller pocket-sized paperbacks within the next ten years or so.

I also don't see a big future for hardcover books simply because they're so expensive. Most people are reluctant to plunk down $30 for a novel, and their reluctance will only increase as e-books redefine price points in the industry. When people become accustomed to paying $2.99 for a new digital book, they'll be much less likely to shell out $30 just to get a print edition. Other than collectible books, art books, and maybe children's books, as well as certain perennial titles or big bestsellers, I think hardcovers will gradually go away.

That leaves you with trade paperbacks - the large-format paperbacks that are already being sold in many venues where you wouldn't have found them five or ten years ago. I think trade paperbacks are the future of print. They will be a mixture of self-published books (mostly print-on-demand), books from the big New York publishers, and books from smaller regional or independent publishers. So in my crystal ball the book marketplace of 15 or 20 years from now consists of e-books and trade paperbacks, with perhaps a few mass-market paperbacks or hardcovers as novelty items.

As far as jobs in the publishing business are concerned, I think you'll see more people working for independent publishers or working as freelance consultants - editors, copy-editors, proofreaders, art designers, layout designers, etc. There will still be jobs in traditional publishing in Manhattan, but that part of the industry will be scaled back, something that's already happening. The more traditional companies have been slow to adapt to changing conditions and are burdened with high overhead and unimaginative business plans. They're going to have to make more significant adjustments then they have so far.

Any other thoughts you would like to share?

In many ways this is the best time I've ever seen to be an author. You are no longer at the mercy of publishers. You are guaranteed to get your book into circulation, at least in digital form. You can publish it for free and potentially reach a wide audience. The downside is that because it's so easy to put out a book, everybody is doing it. You have to find a way to stand out amid the clutter.

Again I would suggest a competitive price, a good cover, good proofreading and layout, and promotional efforts online—not only the Amazon discussion boards, but also Facebook, e-mail, and any other options you can think of. And of course the book itself has to be as good as you can make it. I haven't talked about that, because it's a whole subject in itself.

Self-publishing is by no means a sure thing, but the opportunity is there to find readers and fans, maybe in larger numbers then you ever expected. Good luck!

Author Websites

http://www.michaelprescott.net/

Link to the Author's Amazon Author page

http://www.amazon.com/Michael-Prescott/e/B001IU0L6O/

Terri Reid

Introduction

Mystery writer Terri Reid's love of ghost stories started when she was a toddler and has never waned. She took her destiny into her own hands in August 2010 when she published the first book of her bestselling Mary O'Reilly Paranormal Mystery Series, "Loose Ends". Her seventh book, "Secret Hollows", sold over 8,000 copies in just three weeks! She is currently working on Book 8.

The Interview

Tell us about yourself and your background?

I live in the same area of the United States as my Mary O'Reilly character - Northwest Illinois. I live on five acres of rolling land in a 100 year-old farmhouse, with my husband, children, dogs, cats and several dozen chickens (well, they live in the barn.)

My background is in marketing and public relations, but I have always enjoyed telling stories. For a while, I worked as a freelance journalist for the local paper and wrote the Halloween feature for many years, collecting as many local ghost stories as I could. I gave the collection of ghost stories to the local historical society to use as a fundraiser; they are

GENRE
Paranormal Mystery

now in their third printing.

I don't think you need my whole bio to understand how I got here, but I'd like to offer some relevant points. I did well in high school and received scholarships to go to college. After two years in college, I was married and expecting my first child. College was put on hold. Seven children later, I was working as a consultant doing advertising, marketing and public relations for small to medium-sized businesses in the area. I even had some Fortune 50 companies as clients. I still hadn't found the time to go back to school, but as a consultant, my clients were more interested in what I could do for them, than the degree hanging on the wall - thank goodness!

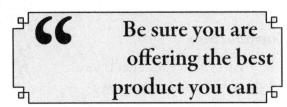

In the background, in my spare time, I was writing novels. It was my dream - "Someday I'm going to be a writer." But, at that point, it was in the same category as "Someday I'm going to be the same size I was when I got married" nice to dream about - but then you wake up!

However, some of the stories had to be told, so, I continued to write. A little every day. While I was writing, I was trying to find my voice and decide what I wanted to write. But, again, since my consulting was paying the bills, writing was more of an escape.

Then the economy crashed and because of the uncertainty of so many things, my clients started tightening their belts and holding on to their money. Marketing budgets were slashed. My business was in trouble. I started looking for a full-time job, but even with fifteen years of experience, I didn't have a degree. And in this job market, employers have lots of options.

Suddenly, the thought of writing for a living made sense, because, really, what did I have to lose?

I had been working on Loose Ends for months. I found

myself with more time than money, so I worked nearly full-time to complete it. During that time, a friend sent me the Wall Street Journal article about Karen McQuestion and her amazing success in e-books. I had heard of Kindles, but I had no idea they held such a market share. I sent an e-mail to Karen, who was gracious enough to answer me. She shared her experiences. Then I did some research on my own and decided that I was going to try downloading my book through Amazon.

Before I learned about Karen, I had planned to send my book off to an agent I had an acquaintance with in New York. She's a very successful agent and, at one time, had told me she liked my writing. But the biggest thing that sold me on e-publishing was the finances. I could get paid within 90 days of downloaded my book. I could make the same amount of money on my e-book that I would through a traditional publisher. And, perhaps, as an entrepreneur this excited me even more; my destiny was in my own hands.

I uploaded Loose Ends on August 3, 2010. I joined some forums and told them about my book. I went on Facebook and told my friends and family about my book and asked them to put my link on their Facebook pages. I called the editor of the

Top Tips from Successful Self-Published Authors

local paper and told him about my book. The paper did a Sunday feature about me and my book. (I had to borrow a Kindle from a friend for the photo!)

In August I sold 142 copies of my book. In September I sold 248 books. In October I added another book, "The Ghosts of New Orleans." I had read that multiple books help you cross market and lead to more sales. The Ghosts of New Orleans was a novel I had written four years ago. It was a darker novel than The Mary O'Reilly stories, but I felt it still had merit. I did a quick edit and uploaded it on October 10th.

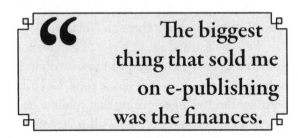
"The biggest thing that sold me on e-publishing was the finances.

In October I sold 789 copies of Loose Ends and 195 copies of The Ghosts of New Orleans.

At the end of November, I added the second Mary O'Reilly book, "Good Tidings." It was available on the night before Thanksgiving. By the end of the month, one week later, I had sold 142 copies of Good Tidings, 745 copies of Loose Ends, and 320 copies of The Ghosts of New Orleans.

In December I watched my numbers climb and three weeks into the month, found that both Loose Ends and Good Tidings had sold over 1,000 copies. I reached those numbers the day after Joe Konrath invited me to be part of his Best Seller blog. I couldn't believe I was part of that crowd of authors. By the end of December, I had sold over 5,000 books.

The information above was part of a blog I wrote in January of 2011. Now, more than a year later, I just uploaded my seventh book in the Mary O'Reilly series – Secret Hollows. In three weeks, the book sold over 8,000 copies and was considered the "#1 Hot New Release" in Women Sleuths for several weeks. I've sold a total of over 280,000 copies of my books. My whole life has changed because of e-publishing.

Loose Ends has been my most popular book– because in April of 2011, I lowered the price to 99 cents. I did this because my books are a series, and even though I only make a minimal amount on Loose Ends, if they like it, they will buy the other books in the series. Loose Ends is also the book I give out for free when I have a chance – for that very same reason. During Christmas of 2011, I offered Loose Ends for free for five days. More than 45,000 people downloaded the book (these numbers were not included in my number above, because they were not books that were sold.) But, my other book numbers jumped tremendously because of the free offer.

Now, the secret to my success is...there is no secret. I've heard rumblings that Paranormal Mysteries or Paranormal Romances are easy to sell. I didn't write my book because of market trends. I wrote it because that was the story I had to tell.

There's been a lot of conversation about quality. You do yourself and this new industry a disservice if you think you can upload something poorly written, poorly edited and poorly executed and try to sell it. Be sure you are offering the best product you can. Don't be your own critic or editor - that never works. Have someone who knows editing - a friend who's a journalist or hire someone - to go through your book. Get some beta-readers to read it and ask them to be honest. It's better they critique your product before you upload it, then afterward say, "Oh, you know, that bothered me a little too."

You only have one chance to make a first impression.

Having a series or getting a new book out soon after the last one is important too. Readers will stay loyal when you give them new offerings. But, if you only upload a book a year or every two years, even those people you impress are going to forget you and your book will sink to the bottom of the very large ocean of Amazon Kindle books. By putting a new book out every three or so months, you make a splash and all of your other books float back up to the top too.

You need to get out there and talk about your book. You are your own marketing and public relations team - if you don't think your book's the greatest thing since sliced bread, why should I?

You need to believe in yourself and write more.

What do you think about the future of the publishing world?

I think many more authors are going to find a way to share their voices in this new e-publishing venue. I think readers are going to become savvier and learn to read samples and not just purchase a book because it's cheap. So, e-publishers are going to have to increase the quality of their work and be able to compete with other very competent writers. I think this is the new revolution of authors who like to have control over their work and control over their future.

Author Websites

http://terrireid.com/

Link to the Author's Amazon Author page

http://www.amazon.com/Terri-Reid/e/B004S8D0R0/

Hugh Howey

Introduction

New York Times bestselling science fiction author Hugh Howey has been self-publishing his work for three years, but his career really took off with the success of his "Wool" novelette in the Fall of 2011. Hugh's fans demanded more stories from the subterranean world he'd created, so Hugh kept writing. In May 2012, the Wool film rights were picked up by Ridley Scott and Steve Zaillian, in partnership with 20th Century Fox.

The Interview

Tell us about yourself and your background?

I've been an avid reader for as long as I can remember. Through my love of books, I've always dreamed of one day becoming a writer. I tried to write novels when I was younger, but I repeatedly gave up after the first few chapters. I lacked the drive to write every single day. So I quit trying to write and resigned myself to reading and reading.

I went to the College of Charleston and studied English, but I never graduated. I was living on a sailboat at the time to save money (and because it felt adventurous). After my junior year, I decided to delay my graduation and go on a long sailing trip. I spent a year

GENRE Science Fiction

in the Bahamas, flitting from island to island, eating whatever I could catch (which was often lobster!). When I ran out of money, I started working on other people's boats, doing odd jobs like changing a mast light or scraping barnacles off the bottom. Anything dangerous or arduous that the owners would rather not do themselves.

When someone asked if I could do a job, no matter what it was, I always said "yes," and then I taught myself how to do it. This habit had a ratcheting effect. Someone asked, and I said I could drive a 40 foot boat, and then I did. Someone asked if I could deliver a 50 foot boat. I figured it wasn't much different than a 40-footer. Within a year, I was captaining 115 foot yachts up and down the Eastern seaboard. I delivered boats from Barbados to Chicago and everywhere in-between. I worked for the rich and famous, and it was rewarding and backbreaking at the same time.

> **Take advice from others as you start out, and help out those who need it.**

When I met my current wife, all of this changed. I no longer wanted to go to sea. Love does this to a sailor. When she took a job in Virginia, I followed. When she moved to the mountains of North Carolina, I went as well. There, far away from the sea, I dreamed of writing again. This time, unlike that youthful spirit who couldn't sit down long enough to finish what he started, I wrote works to completion. I shared them. I gave them away. And when someone asked if I shouldn't be doing this for a living, I said: "Sure. I can do that."

What made you decide to self-publish?

After much cajoling from friends, I decided to query my first manuscript to agents and small publishers. After three weeks of this, I had two small publishers interested. Both were willing to pay a small advance and all the costs of editing and publishing my work. It was a standard contract, with normal terms and rates, and this was already far more than I ever dreamed anyone would offer, so I accepted.

Very quickly, I saw what was involved with publishing a book, all that was expected of me and how much of the profit that meant giving up, and I wondered if I couldn't do it all myself. I would have more freedom and keep a larger share of the proceeds. And so, even though I had a great experience with my publisher, when the second contract arrived in the mail, I decided not to sign it. I went on my own. It's been a blissfully rewarding experience, the difference between renting and owning, between clocking in at a job and running your own small business. The work is greater, but far more self-fulfilling.

How long have you been self-publishing?

Over three years. It feels like longer!

What has been the most effective thing that you have done to promote your book?

I kept writing. This has been the most frustrating learning experience for me: Nothing you can do will sustain sales for your current works quite like writing the next work. My bestselling series took off completely on its own. I didn't even have a link to the book on my website. It was a short piece I wrote and put on the Kindle store, then forgot about. Readers discovered the work and started writing reviews, recommending it to friends and family, and it snowballed. Nothing I've done to promote the book has matched the word-of-mouth from readers. So my advice for selling current works is to keep writing what will eventually become your future ones. When one series takes off, you'll have a deeper library for readers to enjoy. And honestly, the best writing years of my life were when I labored in obscurity, had a day job, and wrote purely for the love of it.

Do you do anything that you consider out of the ordinary to make your book a success?

For Wool, yes. When the first short work gained momentum, I immediately set about writing more works in a serialized fashion. By getting these out swiftly, but with the same quality and style readers were enjoying in the first entry, I captured the groundswell and turned it into an avalanche. The release schedule meant I suddenly had five books in the top-10 lists of some categories on Amazon. This captured the attention of browsers and made them more likely to read synopses and reviews. It was a happy accident, but I truly believe that the release method, this Dickensonian serialization, helped catapult Wool much higher than a single novel would have.

How have you gone about getting the word out about your book?

I try everything, but I'm not sure what actually works. I Tweet and blog; I post on Facebook; I participate on forums and do interviews. The biggest bumps I've had in sales have come from major reviews like on BoingBoing.net and Wired.com, from huge media mentions like a half page story in Entertainment Weekly or the piece in Variety, and from the news of my film rights being picked up by Ridley Scott. With each of these, I could watch the increase in sales. Nothing else has had that distinct boost, but I imagine the culmination of all my efforts help keep sales where they are.

What has been your most successful self-published book, and how many have you sold?

The Wool Omnibus, which collects the five stories in a single volume, has been my runaway bestseller. It hit the New York Times charts and the USA Today bestseller list and has spent three straight months in the Amazon top 100. Across the Wool series, I've sold over 150,000 copies. And while I'm independent here in the States, I've been picked up in a dozen foreign countries, including the UK, where Random House has a hardback release planned for January. It's flabbergasting, frankly. It all started with a 12,000 word novelette. And now Ridley Scott and Random House have scooped up various facets of the rights. Honestly, none of this has truly sunk in. I'm just staggering around in a dreamlike state. I keep writing, and I keep expecting to wake up.

What are your top tips for new indie authors?

Write, write, write. Do it every single day. Don't be afraid of the blank page or the next chapter. Just sink into your character's mind and describe the world and conflict in which they find themself. And be patient. It took me three years to make anything appreciable. It can take twice that long. But if you can release three or four works a year that are well-edited and enjoyable, good things will happen. I don't believe this simply because it happened to me. I've preached this all along.

What do you think about the future of the publishing world?

I'm excited! Readers will have a greater selection at a lower price. Authors will have more avenues for success and an easier path to publication. The royalty rates are top-notch. The costs are minimal. There's never been a better time, in the history of mankind, to be a storyteller. Never. And this isn't just a goldrush. Don't believe that tripe. This is the flowering dreams of millions of aspiring writers, just like I was when I was a boy, but with a difference: Now there is a chance to have your words widely read. This has never been true before. The reason you're seeing so many people produce works for the first time is because they can, not simply because they are trying to get rich quick (which is the wrong reason to pursue writing, in my opinion).

Any other thoughts you would like to share?

To writers: Be good to one another. The tide is rising, and it will lift all ships. This isn't a competition or a war; it's a brotherhood. A sisterhood. The more we turn people onto reading, the more all of our works will be read. Take advice from others as you start out, and help out those who need it as you gain your own footing. Writing is hard. There's no reason to make it harder on each other.

To readers: It is all for you. Your feedback means everything. If you finish a book that moves you, fire off an e-mail to the author, however big or small they might be. Write a review. Tell a friend. Our success, I've learned, hinges on how much you enjoy what we produce and what you do after you read that last page. That means half of our success is up to us. The rest? It's up to you.

Author Websites

http://www.hughhowey.com/

Link to the Author's Amazon Author page

http://www.amazon.com/Hugh-Howey/e/B002RX4S5Q/

Scott Nicholson

Introduction

Author Scott Nicholson has written bestselling thrillers, short stories, comics series, children's books, YA paranormal fantasies, screenplays and collaborated with other indie authors on "The Indie Journey: Secrets to Writing Success". "Liquid Fear" was published in December 2011 and has sold over 100,000 copies so far. Scott has had an incredible journey!

The Interview

Tell us about yourself and your background?

I was raised a poor country boy and imagination had to do where money couldn't. Having some blank paper and crayons always gave me a rush, even from the very beginning. Of course, that's probably how I will go out, too, doodling and drooling.

What made you decide to self-publish?

I'd been through publishers and agents and as the industry got tougher, I still kept writing even through rejection. I saw an opportunity to meet readers, and I took the step, and soon grew more confident as I found most of the things I enjoyed were perfect for the digital era.

GENRE
Supernatural Thriller

How long have you been self-publishing?

About two and a half years now. It gets more fun and better all the time, with new opportunities arising.

What has been the most effective thing that you have done to promote your book?

I believe in a mix of social media and paid advertising, constantly trying new things.

> "I do a lot of giveaways, what I call "generosity marketing."

I also do a lot of giveaways, what I call "generosity marketing." I've probably helped give away 40 Kindle Fires by now, and approaching a million free books distributed.

Do you do anything that you consider out of the ordinary to make your book a success?

I like to cultivate friendships with my readers, and the giveaways are one way to reward the people who have supported me. A writer only gets as far as the readers will take him. And writers also spend more time, cumulatively, than the writer does.

How have you gone about getting the word out about your book?

Advertising and sponsorships, as well as giving away books. I am a partner in the book-promotion and giveaway site e-bookSwag.com, which is built on many of the successful principles I've used in building my foundation.

What has been your most successful self-published book, and how many have you sold?

Liquid Fear sold about 80,000 copies and was picked up by Amazon's Thomas & Mercer imprint and is well over 100,000 copies sold by now. I've had a few that have done pretty well and some that are taking longer to find their audience.

What are your top tips for new indie authors?

Focus on excellence in every area. Be a professional, commit to the craft, and be distinct. People who follow the crowd get stuck in the crowd when the crowd stops. Better to be the outlier, the weird one, what Seth Godin calls the "purple cow." Be yourself, because that is what the world needs.

What do you think about the future of the publishing world?

I believe e-books are the future, and the future is arriving faster than anyone would have us believe. I foresee the lending library or subscription model as the dominant delivery system, and free books supported by sponsorships or advertisers. Really, there is no reason for an e-book to be $10 or $15 except for greed. A digital product is virtually free to distribute, so every other cost is artificial. And, yes, the writer's time is a subjective and artificial cost, no matter what they like to believe.

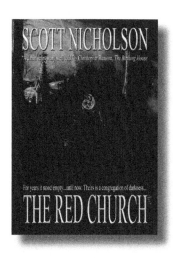

Any other thoughts you would like to share?

    I am so joyful to see this new era and so many creative people taking responsibility for their lives and careers, using their talents to communicate and share ideas. I don't think we'll all end up as the legendary "Kindle millionaires," but it beats the hell out of working.

Author Websites

http://www.hauntedcomputer.com/
http://e-bookSwag.com/

Link to the Author's Amazon Author page

http://www.amazon.com/Scott-Nicholson/e/B001HCX30O/

Kristen Ashley

Introduction

Kristen Ashley has written a total of thirty-one books, including the Rock Chick Series, the Colorado Mountain Series, the Burg Series, the Dream Man Series and the Fantasyland Series, and covering various genres. Kristen's books always include humor, romance and engaging characters.

The Interview

Tell us about yourself and your background?

I've been writing for ten years, self-publishing for four. I have thirty-one books published in e-book, three in print. And I'm living my dream.

What made you decide to self-publish?

Ten years ago, I attempted to find an agent and/or publisher and found the process extremely time-consuming, stressful, expensive and, in the end, disheartening. Although happy to go that route when I was "ready", by the time I was fully ready, self-publishing was a viable option. And it isn't any of those things (except, if you publish in print, the expensive part).

GENRE
Romance

How long have you been self-publishing?

For four years but only just over one in e-books.

What has been the most effective thing that you have done to promote your book?

My website. Absolutely. I had it professionally done, made a great deal of information available including sample chapters of books and infused it with my personality. I don't know why, exactly, but it established my credibility as a writer. Even family and friends who knew I'd been writing and publishing for years didn't take me seriously until I launched my website. Though, I will admit it isn't inexpensive and it remains time-consuming as it's important to keep it up-to-date and ever-changing so folks will want to come back time and again to see what's new.

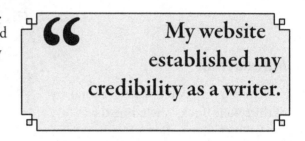

Do you do anything that you consider out of the ordinary to make your book a success?

Even looking back, I'm not certain I'd recommend this but I purposefully did not pay attention to what other writers, self-published or not, did to promote their books. I did this because I didn't want to be a copycat or sway the way I approached things. There are strong, underlying messages in all my books about the power of women and accepting yourself for who you are. So, I wanted to put myself forward with that message. I wanted to try to be unique and have my voice ring true to who I am and therefore establish what a reader could expect. Indeed, I am an extension of my books and I wanted to communicate that. This led to me making some mistakes and being late to the game on some things. But, in the end, it worked! Though, it did take longer.

How have you gone about getting the word out about your book?

Social media. I have a Facebook page that I religiously visit at least once a day and I commune with my readers there. And love every second. This is mostly about my books or things that interest me. I have a Twitter account where I promote books and blogs, etc. but also it's a bit more personal as to whatever's on my mind or happening in my life. I have a Goodreads page/account and I publish blogs there as well as on my website. Also there, I communicate with readers. I've already mentioned the website which I try very hard to keep up-to-date when time allows. I have Amazon Author pages. I never turn down interviews from bloggers, ever! Blog reviewers have been extremely helpful in promoting my work but also doing the interviews is a blast! And I have done on-line chats with readers. This last is a blast as well and I recommend it to all writers. It's a thrill to communicate real-time with readers. Though, I will caution that it gets a little crazy so you should have someone moderating it in order that you don't miss answering questions.

What has been your most successful self-published book?

Sweet Dreams of my Colorado Mountain series.

What are your top tips for new indie authors?

1. When you write, be true to you, your voice and tell your story. And be sure to have your book proofread (at least) then publish!
2. Although you should get feedback and process it, don't write by committee. You will never make everyone happy.
3. Create a good website, become a member of Goodreads and make a Facebook page for yourself. And as with #1, be yourself in all these places.
4. Give time and attention to blog reviewers. They are passionate about reading, they're awesome people and even if they don't like every part of your work or give you a less than favorable review, they are still spreading the word.
5. And last but tied for first, treat your readers as they are. Precious. Reply to their e-mails and give them your time. Not all of it or you'd never have time to write. But if they take the time out of their busy lives to share they enjoy your work, you should be certain to let them know how much you appreciate it. I have made certain to do this and it has enriched my life. Many of my readers are now friends and you can never have enough friends! This is an unexpected bounty when folks find your work. So carve time out for it, you won't be sorry.

What do you think about the future of the publishing world?

I think with self-publishing, it's opening up and if more readers will embrace self-published authors, they'll experience the beauty of that. I belonged to a writer's website prior to publishing and the work I read on there was as good as if not better than stuff I'd read published by traditional publishers. And most of it was phenomenal. I'm not joking, most of it! I couldn't believe some of these folks hadn't been picked up!

Any other thoughts you would like to share?

Well, not thoughts just mistakes I've made which, in knowing, might be useful to writers.

Firstly, readers notice mistakes in books and most of my books were published without professional editing. This is expensive and I couldn't afford it but readers picked up on it and they find it annoying. And shared this. I, myself, noticed errors in traditionally published books and I know a bestselling author who also notes that her readers have noticed errors. Therefore, I'm not certain every error can be caught. But I now have a proofreader and feel better about what I publish. I would suggest if you can't afford an editor or proofreader, that you find someone who has good grammar and attention to detail and buy them a bottle of wine so they'll edit your book for you. At least one other set of eyes can make all the difference.

Secondly, reviews are sometimes difficult to take. I mention earlier about not writing by committee. That doesn't mean it isn't crucial to get feedback from your readers about what they like or don't. So do your best to develop a stiff upper lip. I have taken comments from reviews and used it to better my writing. I've even gotten ideas for plots from reviewers! I don't scour my reviews and often avoid them but when I'm feeling strong, I will take a look so I can absorb what my readers are thinking. If one, two or even five people dislike the same thing, that doesn't mean you need to change the way you do what you do. But if there are things that are repeated frequently, you need to consider it.

And lastly, there are forums where folks discuss books. Some may argue with me but I would strongly suggest leaving readers to their discussions and do not, ever, get on those and push your books. They want to talk about books and recommend books and they usually have established very strong communities. This is an intrusion. They might not mention it but many dislike it.

And I say this because I did just this. It made me uncomfortable, I did it with one book and stopped. And, although I know one or two folks read my book, it isn't worth it to intrude in their communities. This is simply my opinion but there you go. And also, on forums, there will be entire topics where you can promote your work that is dedicated to that so it is expected. I would suggest you leave your messages there and only there.

Author Websites

http://www.kristenashley.net/
http://www.facebook.com/pages/Kristen-Ashley/83283039199
http://www.goodreads.com/author/show/2958084.Kristen_Ashley

Link to the Author's Amazon Author page

http://www.amazon.com/Kristen-Ashley/e/B002D68GBY/

Aaron Patterson

Introduction

Aaron Patterson is known for his bestselling thrillers, the WJA series featuring protagonist Mark Appleton, and his new YA paranormal Airel saga.

He founded the StoneHouse Ink indie publishing house which Aaron describes as "a mild mannered publishing house by day and a superhero by night". As well as publishing, it offers resources for authors, such as classes and webinars.

Aaron's blog, The Worst Book Ever, is well worth following for indie publishing advice with a touch of humor.

The Interview

Tell us about yourself and your background?

I was home-schooled and grew up in the west. I worked construction for 11 years and owned a small construction company. I wrote my first book in 2008 and spent a year researching publishing. It did not take me long to see it is one big fat mess! Thus, I started my own publishing house. In November of 2009 StoneHouse Ink was born. We now have 40 authors and around 10 bestsellers. I am also the co-founder of The Idaho Book Extravaganza and StoneHouse University.

GENRE
Thrillers / YA Romance

What made you decide to self-publish?

I did not want to spend my time trying to find a publisher when in the same amount of time I could publish and start selling my own books. Some writers spend three years or more just trying to get an agent, in that time I have 5 books published and am a full time writer.

> **" I look at the New York Times bestsellers and try to compete with them.**

How long have you been self-publishing?

As of December of 2008.

What has been the most effective thing that you have done to promote your book?

Social media such as Facebook, Twitter and my blog.

Do you do anything that you consider out of the ordinary to make your book a success?

I look at the New York Times bestsellers and try to compete with them, not the other self-published authors. I want to go head to head with Dean Koontz and James Patterson.

How have you gone about getting the word out about your book?

Through social media. The key is to be yourself and be nice. Most authors pound their books down the throats of everyone unlucky enough to stumble on their Facebook profile. It is better to just be nice, everyone knows I have a book; I do not need to tell them.

Aaron Patterson

What has been your most successful self-published book, and how many have you sold?

Sweet Dreams, my first in the Mark Appleton series is my bestselling book. I am up to 200k copies and growing. Just last month (March 2012) I sold over 20K copies between 4 titles just on Amazon.

What are your top tips for new indie authors?

Learn, Learn and Learn! Take classes, study, watch, and become the best at what you do. Don't jump on all the quick sales junk or think of this as anything but a marathon.

What do you think about the future of the publishing world?

I think is it dang exciting! I mean, we have so much still in front of us; you can look at the huge wave coming and run and hide or grab your surf board! Hang loose.

Any other thoughts you would like to share?

Be nice. That is all.

Author Websites

http://theworstbookever.blogspot.com/

Link to the Author's Amazon Author page

http://www.amazon.com/Aaron-Patterson/e/B002O5G9AE/

Carol Luce Davis

Introduction

Bestselling author Carol Davis Luce is know for her five suspense novels, her two short story collections and her villains, who are "evil personified". Her skill at building suspense in her novels has led to her contributing two articles to Writer's Digest.

The Interview

Tell us about yourself and your background?

I wasn't born to write. Writing came to me later in life, channeled through my devoted interest in books. As a voracious reader, I felt something was missing in the novels I loved to read. I wanted more. After searching unsuccessfully for novels to satisfy my balance of romance, suspense and intrigue, I realized I had to write that book myself. Two years later, NIGHT STALKER was finished. Followed by five other 'Night' books.

What made you decide to self-publish?

With five published novels under my belt, when the sixth failed to find a home, I took time out to write a fictionalized memoir. I also signed on as a writing instructor for Writer's Digest. After several years of teaching novel workshops

GENRE
Suspense

for advanced writers, I had become quite content to put my own career on hold to help other aspiring writers succeed.

Fast-forward fifteen years to 2010. My best buddy, J. Carson Black, made the move into self-publishing first. (Her success with her traditionally published thrillers published as e-books has been phenomenal. Black's self-published, THE SHOP, is a bestseller, and her Laura Cardinal mysteries were recently optioned by Winkler/Sony for a TV series.)

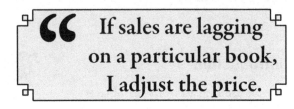

She encouraged me to join the twenty-first century. When the publisher copyrights to my suspense novels expired and those rights reverted to me, I converted the five novels into digital format. Out-of-print and used books bring in no royalties for the author. I figured that revenue I made from the newly published e-books would be more than I'd made in over a decade, so I was optimistic, and eager to see them available to readers again.

How long have you been self-publishing?

My first independent (Indie) novel, NIGHT WIDOW, was published in 2011. Two short story anthologies, BROKEN JUSTICE and FOR BETTER, FOR WORSE, were released in 2012.

Note: As an added bonus, when my former agent noticed the astonishing bump in e-book sales for my suspense novel, NIGHT PASSAGE, a novel he represents through another Print on Demand/Digital publisher, he offered to shop NIGHT WIDOW to the Big 6. I graciously declined. I no longer have the patience for the grueling submission dance and, should it sell, the long book production process. I like being in charge. If the book tanks, I have no one to blame but myself.

What has been the most effective thing that you have done to promote your book?

I attribute my success to luck and good timing. I entered the game just prior to when the e-book market burst wide open. I had multiple books to offer, which increases exposure. I kept the price at $3.99. It was slow going for the first six months, with book sales averaging about 100 a month. In August of 2011, I followed John Locke's .99 cent strategy for success and lowered the price of my books to .99 cents at a time when .99 cents was the going price to attract attention for bargain hunters and avid readers. Sales took off! My books began to show up on category Top 100 lists. Five months later, in January of 2012, I had sold 100,000 e-books. Two novels, NIGHT GAME and NIGHT STALKER, made it onto the Kindle Store Bestseller list. NIGHT GAME reached #7 in the Kindle Indie Authors Bestseller List. Today, FREE is the bargain price. (Even this is changing. Offering your books for free isn't what it was before Amazon introduced Kindle Direct Publishing Select (KDP SELECT) and flooded the market with free books in late 2011.)

Do you do anything that you consider out of the ordinary to make your book a success?

I vary the price of my books, starting at .99 cents upwards of $4.99. If sales are lagging on a particular book, I adjust the price. I don't give my books away anymore, but I will offer a sale for several days and promote the sale on Facebook and Twitter. I revamp the book covers and punch up the product description on the title pages. I add the appropriate 'tags' on my title pages to insure that the search engines can find it. This process is ongoing.

What about paid advertising or paid promotions?

It doesn't work for me. I don't know why, but it seems to work against me.

How have you gone about getting the word out about your book?

My Blogsite and Author Website. Social networks such as Facebook and Twitter, though I'm careful to not be pushy. No one likes a pushy salesperson. I'm a member of several writers' groups and participate in their various anthologies and promotions where book proceeds go to charity. The Indie Chicks Cafe rocks! This group of talented indie writers are supportive and just plain awesome. Visit them at http://indiechickscafe.com/

What has been your most successful self-published book, and how many have you sold?

NIGHT GAME. Over 50,000 sold in 8 months. It reached #29 on the Kindle Store Bestseller list (that's #29 out of 1 million Amazon books).

What are your top tips for new indie authors?

Before you put that wonderful book out there for the world to see, enlist several beta readers to make sure it's market ready. Pay to have it properly formatted. Pay a copy-editor to dot the i's and cross the t's. Design a stunning book cover, or hire someone to design it for you. Write a product description that hooks the reader--make it sing. Oh, one more thing: write a damn good book.

What do you think about the future of the publishing world?

There will always be books and readers to read them. Digital books are here to stay. Paper books continue to thrive as well. Consider self-publishing in both digital and POD (Print on Demand) format. NIGHT WIDOW, my latest release, is now in paperback along with NIGHT PASSAGE.

Any other thoughts you would like to share?

If you are a writer, now's your chance to become a bona fide author. The beauty of self-publishing is that nothing in digital format is written in stone. You get 'do-overs' if something needs to be changed. Even traditionally published books, when converted to digital format, develop conversion glitches and must be fixed. Readers will notice and some will comment with a bad review. I have re-edited all of my e-books and changed or enhanced the book covers. It's a whole new publishing world out there. If you're willing to work hard and keep on top of the constant changes, it's yours for the taking!

Author Websites

http://caroldavisluce.com/
http://imagerystudios.com/carol

Link to the Author's Amazon Author page

http://www.amazon.com/Carol-Davis-Luce/e/B000APHQU2/

Claire Ridgway

Introduction

Claire Ridgway has been writing all her life but came to self-publishing via a different route than many indie authors: through blogging. Little did she know that blogging about Tudor history would lead to success as a non-fiction indie author. Claire self-published her first book in February 2012, followed, just two months, later by her second book. She's enjoying every minute of the indie journey and blogs regularly at www.interviewswithindieauthors.com.

The Interview

Tell us about yourself and your background?

I started my working life as a teacher but gave up to be a stay-at-home mother. When my children started school, I wanted to work from home and as I had always written as a hobby I decided to do freelance writing. In February 2009, I started The Anne Boleyn Files website, combining my two passions: Tudor history and writing. By the summer of 2009, the website had become so popular that I decided to concentrate full-time on my history research and writing.

GENRE: Non-Fiction - History

What made you decide to self-publish?

Fast forward to 2011. I was working on various book projects and was in contact with an agent who was very interested in one of my book proposals, but deemed others "not commercially viable". While I was working on my proposals, one of my regular website visitors asked me to publish some of my most popular articles as a celebration of the upcoming 3rd birthday of The Anne Boleyn Files. I asked some of my other regulars what they thought and they all loved the idea, so The Anne Boleyn Collection was born. I didn't even bother talking to the agent, as I knew nobody would be interested in publishing a collection of blog articles. I researched self-publishing and decided to publish my book through CreateSpace and Kindle Direct Publishing. It was released in February 2012 and quickly became a bestseller. I was astonished as I thought only die-hard fans of The Anne Boleyn Files would be interested in it.

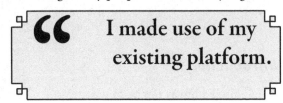
I made use of my existing platform.

My next project was a countdown of the events leading up to Anne Boleyn's execution in May 1536. I knew this would interest people because I'd always done a countdown on the website. I chose to self-publish again as I wanted it out quickly, in time for 19th May 2012, and also because I knew that a traditional publisher would want me to change its diary format. The whole point of the book was to be a countdown, one day at a time, so that it was easy to digest and so that people could dip into it. I didn't want to change it. I released it in April 2012 and by mid June 2012 it had sold over 4500 copies.

How long have you been self-publishing?

Since February 2012.

What has been the most effective thing that you have done to promote your book?

I made use of my existing platform. When I released my first book in February 2012, I already had:
- A website attracting nearly 25,000 people a month
- A list of over 5,000 subscribers
- A Facebook following of nearly 5,000
- Over 3,000 Twitter followers

Plus, I had a YouTube channel and I had built up relationships with historians, authors and other history bloggers. I already had a platform to market my book to, so it was easy to get a buzz going and to get the news of my book releases out there.

Another thing which really worked for my second book was listing it for free for two days on Amazon, using KDP select. I had nearly 27,000 downloads in 48 hours and it had a dramatic impact on sales in the following weeks, plus I shot to No.2 on the Top 100 Free Kindle Books. I didn't just list it and sit back though, I advertised it on all the Kindle websites and announced it to all my lists and followers.

Do you do anything that you consider out of the ordinary to make your book a success?

Two things:
1. I did virtual book tours. Shortly after the release date of both my books, I arranged to write guest articles or do interviews on other history blogs, and I also gave prizes. I announced the tour schedule on my website and also the book websites, and then I reminded people where I was each day. This was a great way of promoting my book to different audiences and also of saying thank you to the history blogging community. It was a win-win situation for everyone involved – I got publicity and the bloggers got free content and their blog introduced to new visitors.

2. I blog regularly on The Anne Boleyn Files and write daily posts on Facebook and Twitter. I interact with my followers and readers, giving free information and interesting tit-bits. I'm also available to my readers and followers, in that they can email me and I respond. I love getting to know people and answering their questions.

How have you gone about getting the word out about your book?

Via my platform – my website, book trailers on my YouTube channel, emails to my subscribers, Amazon links on my website, announcements on Twitter and Facebook. Other Tudor history bloggers were also kind enough to spread the news on their blogs and to host me on their blogs on my virtual book tours.

With my second book, The Fall of Anne Boleyn: A Countdown, I did an interactive time-line and published snippets from my book each day counting down to Anne Boleyn's execution. This gave people a taster of what the book was about.

What has been your most successful self-published book, and how many have you sold?

As of 8th July 2012, I have sold over 14,000 books. The Anne Boleyn Collection has sold 8000, but that was in five months, so I'd say that my most successful book is The Fall of Anne Boleyn because it has sold over 6000 in less than 3 months.

What are your top tips for new indie authors?

Build a platform. I put my success down to the three years of work I had done beforehand. It was all accidental, in a way, because I hadn't purposely built that platform with a book in mind, but it was there when I needed it. You can't just release a book and hope that people will just stumble across it on Amazon, you need a way of reaching potential readers. Start blogging about your subject, your self-publishing journey, your book ideas or characters, anything! Be committed to blogging regularly and doing something each day to get the word out about your book.

Also, get your book professionally edited and hire a cover designer. People do judge books by the covers, it's hard not to when a reader is shopping on Amazon. Readers also hate bad grammar and spelling mistakes; errors distract them from your story. Don't give self-publishing a bad name, make your book a quality product.

Develop 'rhino skin', as I call it. You will get bad reviews and some will be downright nasty. You can't please everyone and not everyone is going to love you and your book, it's the way of the world. Read the review, consider whether any of the points are valid and need working on, then read your best review and move on. Go and read the bad reviews of your favorite author, that might cheer you up!

It's so easy to let the negativity and doubt seep in and stop you in your tracks, but don't let it get to you. You need a thick skin if you're going to put your work out there to be judged by the world.

Top Tips from Successful Self-Published Authors

What do you think about the future of the publishing world?

It's changing! I don't believe that traditional publishing is dead, but I do believe that publishers need to move with the times. I turned down a publishing contract recently for three reasons: 1) It didn't make financial sense with regards to the advance and royalties, 2) The publisher was concerned with hardback sales and not e-book sales, and 3) The distribution was very limited and print runs were small. Why would an author limit themselves like this?

Any other thoughts you would like to share?

There is no magic answer. I'm always being asked what the secret is to the success of my website and books, as if there is some kind of magic secret or ingredient. It's like people who look for 'get rich quick' schemes. Either people think I have some kind of secret or they put it down to luck. Success in self-publishing is not about luck, it's about hard work and about treating it as a business. I research, write and blog every day and I work silly hours, but I love what I do and wouldn't have it any other way. My work is my passion and that drives me.

Author Websites

http://www.claireridgway.com/
http://www.theanneboleynfiles.com/
https://twitter.com/AnneBoleynFiles
http://www.facebook.com/pages/Claire-Ridgway/396222483770661

Link to the Author's Amazon Author page

http://www.amazon.com/Claire-Ridgway/e/B0079FOGUY/

Alexa Grace

Introduction

Romantic suspense author Alexa Grace is the author of the bestselling Deadly Trilogy. She has only been self-publishing since Christmas 2011 but has been highly successful, putting her success down to writing riveting books and interacting with her fans.

The Interview

Tell us about yourself and your background?

I have a Bachelor's degree in Communication and a Master's in Education from Indiana State University in Terre Haute, Indiana. I directed training and development departments for corporations for the bulk of my career.

My journey as an indie author started in March 2011 when the Sr. Director of Training and Development position I'd held for thirteen years was eliminated. A door closed for me but another one opened. I finally had the time to pursue my dream of writing books - my dream since childhood. My focus is now on writing riveting romantic suspense novels that take my readers on a wild, hot ride.

GENRE
Romantic Suspense

What made you decide to self-publish?

I did a lot of Internet research in self-publishing after I lost my job, and read a lot of books. The more I learned about it, the more determined I was to self-publish. Indie authors like Theresa Ragan and John Locke really motivated me to take the indie route. Like them, I wanted to retain control of book design, writing, marketing, etc. The indie journey has been filled with new learning experiences and relationships that have fortified me as an author and human being. I made the right decision.

How long have you been self-publishing?

Almost seven months. My first book was published on Christmas Day 2011 as a gift to myself.

What has been the most effective thing that you have done to promote your book?

I spent a lot of time using social media to promote my books. Facebook and Twitter have been great marketing options for me.

Do you do anything that you consider out of the ordinary to make your books a success?

Early in my indie journey, I pledged to stay close to my readers and listen to them. What I've heard from them lately (loud and clear) is that they want me to continue the Deadly Trilogy series adding characters, relationships, mystery and suspenseful adventures. Although that was not my initial plan, that is exactly what I am going to do. I agree with my readers. I love reading books in a series, too. You fall in love with the characters and don't want the story to end.

I had no idea that I would enjoy hearing from readers as much as I do. An email from one of them has the potential to make my day.

My readers mean a lot to me. I want readers to finish the last chapter of one of my books, sit back and think, "Wow, that book was a fun, wild ride with hot romance, thrilling suspense with a dash of humor."

I want readers to enjoy reading the book as much as I enjoyed writing it. If I succeed in doing that, my books will be a success.

How have you gone about getting the word out about your book?

In addition to using social media, I advertise on various reader websites. I also send an e-newsletter discussing upcoming releases, free book alerts and my indie journey to a list of readers and friends that grow each day. I love hearing from readers so I have a good author website that enables readers to communicate with me. In addition, I make it easy for readers to write to me by listing my email address freely.

What has been your most successful self-published book, and how many have you sold?

Deadly Deception has taken off like a rocket. The book was launched on June 1, 2012, and is already on Amazon's Top 100 Bestselling Romantic Suspense Books. At this writing, it is #26. In its first month of sales, it has sold 90% more books than Deadly Offerings' first month.

What are your top tips for new indie authors?

1. One of the wisest things I did as an indie author was to join an online group of indie romance authors that was suggested to me by Theresa Ragan. This group of wonderful, supportive authors have taught me so much. I

am eternally grateful for their support and willingness to share information and wisdom.

2. John Locke's e-book How I sold 1 Million e-books in Five Months was very helpful and I recommend it to new indie authors.

3. Don't let bad reviews get you down. Every time I get a bad review, I get out my favorite quote by John Locke. "They buy your book for different reasons: they may like the cover. It has lots of great reviews. It's a bestseller. And these readers will love it, hate it, or forget it. If they love it, you've got another fan. If they hate it, they blame you and the folks who gave you a good rating. Doesn't mean your book sucks, and it doesn't mean they're petty, hateful people. It simply means they aren't part of your target audience."

What do you think about the future of the publishing world?

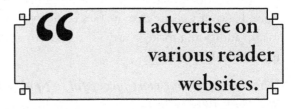

I think traditional publishers have had a good run. They've had the ultimate control of authors and books for a long, long time. I predict they will be adjusting to more and more change in their industry that will impact their bottom line. Digital publishing is our future.

Any other thoughts you would like to share?

There is a sign that hangs in my office that says, "You are the author of your own life story". I believe this to be true. If your dream is to become an indie author, make it happen. Start today. Life is too short to procrastinate when it comes to your dreams.

Author Websites

http://www.alexa-grace.net/

Link to the Author's Amazon Author page

http://www.amazon.com/Alexa-Grace/e/B006QKYVB2/

Marie Force

Introduction

Award-winning and bestselling romance novelist Marie Force has been self-publishing since November 2010 and has self-published a total of thirteen books, including the popular McCarthys of Gansett Island Series. Marie also helps other indie authors with her E-Book Formatting Fairies business.

The Interview

Tell us about yourself and your background?

I've been a working writing and editor for my entire professional career, including a 16-year stint as communication director for a national membership organization where I served as editor-in-chief of a trade magazine. As of January 1st of this year (and thanks solely to self-publishing) I'm a full-time author with 21 books available and many more coming. Thirteen of my books are self-published and eight are traditionally published. My Fatal Series, a romantic suspense series set in Washington, D.C., is published with Harlequin's Carina Press and HQN in paperback. I live in Rhode Island with my husband of 20 years, two teenagers and two frisky dogs.

GENRE: Romance

What made you decide to self-publish?

I wrote seven books before I sold one, and I never gave up on those earlier books. After I was traditionally published, I had readers asking for more, I had books my publisher wasn't interested in and a way to get them to readers thanks to the Kindle, Nook, iPad, Kobo, etc. It was a match made in heaven!

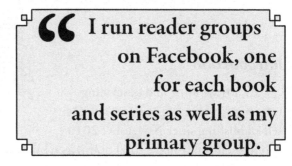

How long have you been self-publishing?

I self-published my first book, True North, in November 2010. Twelve other books followed in quick succession. All of my self-published books are original work that has never before been published.

What has been the most effective thing that you have done to promote your book?

Write and publish the next book. I believe the best way to build a readership and a following is to keep the content coming. I'm lucky to be somewhat prolific and a relatively fast writer. That combination has helped to quickly build my following along with a significant presence on Facebook and a growing presence on Twitter. I run 24 reader groups on Facebook (one for each book and series as well as the primary group, Marie Force Book Talk) that keep me in daily contact with my readers, which has also helped to build my following. I'm known for being "down on the street" with my readers, and I love that interaction. Their feedback has given me ideas for books I had no plans to write—until they asked for them. I like to give the people what they want!

Do you do anything that you consider out of the ordinary to make your book a success?

I can't think of anything out of the ordinary beyond keeping the books coming as quickly as possible while keeping quality at the forefront at all times.

How have you gone about getting the word out about your book?

All the usual avenues: Facebook, Twitter, mailing list, blog, website. I've also benefited from word-of-mouth publicity between and among readers. They often tell me they've told all their friends about me. You can't pay for that kind of publicity.

What has been your most successful self-published book, and how many have you sold?

Maid for Love, book 1 in my McCarthys of Gansett Island Series, has been my bestseller with about 70,000 e-books sold so far and counting. It continues to perform very well for me each month more than a year after publication.

What are your top tips for new indie authors?

    Write the best possible books you can, have them edited by a professional copy-editor and story editor (if you need one). If you can't afford a story editor, get some really good beta readers who know how to identify flaws in a story and then LISTEN to them. I am a professional copy-editor and I wouldn't DARE publish a book without another professional copy-editor's blessing. I'm always amazed by the stuff I miss in my own books. While I believe quality is job one for all authors, for the self-published author "quantity" should be job two. Keeping the books coming helps to build buzz and a following. But it all comes back to the books. If they are good, well-written, professionally edited books, you will most likely find your audience. If they are not well written or professionally edited, readers will let you know that with low ratings that can be quite harmful to building your following. Never forget that readers pay attention to feedback from other readers.

What do you think about the future of the publishing world?

    I wouldn't dare to speculate other than to say I think the changes are just beginning. I'm delighted that authors are now able to take control of their own careers and shape their own destinies without having to rely on traditional gatekeepers who were solely responsible for deciding what readers got to read - and what they didn't get to read. It's thrilling to see authors in a position of power, even if it's only over their own careers. That is a "sea" change, and one that was long overdue in my opinion.

Any other thoughts you would like to share?

One of the most exciting things I've gotten to do is help other authors get their books ready for self-publication. My E-book Formatting Fairies business has really taken off as more and more authors choose to take the self-publishing path. The technology behind e-book publication can be daunting. The Fairies wave a wand, and it is done! That's been a lot of fun and very satisfying.

Author Websites

http://www.mariesullivanforce.com/
http://e-bookformattingfairies.blogspot.com/

Link to the Author's Amazon Author page

http://www.amazon.com/Marie-Force/e/B001JS34LY/

Shadonna Richards

Introduction

Romance author Shadonna Richard sold over 45,000 e-books in the first eight months after the release of her first novel, "An Unexpected Bride" (Book 1 in the Bride Series), and three of her Bride Series novels simultaneously occupied the Top 5 Hot New Releases in Romance Anthologies in May 2012. All of her romance novels (to date) have hit the #1 spot in their categories. These are incredible achievements for a new author.

The Interview

Tell us about yourself and your background?

I have a degree in Psychology and a Nursing Diploma. I enjoy reading and writing about the magic of romance and the power of love.

What made you decide to self-publish?

After collecting 200 rejections from agents and publisher during the course of five years on a variety of projects I submitted, I decided, after reading about Amanda Hocking, to hire a good editor, polish my work, and upload my stories on Kindle.

How long have you been self-publishing?

I've been self-publishing on Kindle for one year now and have sold more than 75,000 e-books in the first year on Kindle.

What has been the most effective thing that you have done to promote your book?

Joining Kindleboards.com and sharing and learning so much from the wonderful authors and readers there. In addition to that, getting the word out through wonderful book review bloggers. I went through Bewitching Book Tours initially and the results have been phenomenal.

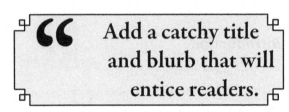

> Add a catchy title and blurb that will entice readers.

Do you do anything that you consider out of the ordinary to make your book a success?

I write books that I'm passionate about and have chosen to write in the genre that I love to read.

How have you gone about getting the word out about your book?

In addition to what I mentioned above relating to promoting my book, I also sponsored posts on Kindle Nation Daily, Kindle Fire Department, Ereader News Today and Pixel of Ink to help by getting exposure to their awesome readers.

What has been your most successful self-published book, and how many have you sold?

An Unexpected Bride (Book 1 in the Bride Series) which has sold over 45,000 copies in its first eight months of release on Amazon alone!!!

What are your top tips for new indie authors?

Enjoy what you're doing. Write what you love to read. Tell a great story. Hire a good editor. Get a great cover for your book. Add a catchy title and blurb that will entice readers and above all, keep writing and keep honing your skills.

What do you think about the future of the publishing world?

Let's just say that I spend more time downloading books on my Kindle than purchasing books in a book store.

Any other thoughts you would like to share?

Work hard, rest well, interact with others and believe in yourself.

Author Websites

http://www.shadonnarichards.blogspot.com/

Link to the Author's Amazon Author page

http://www.amazon.com/Shadonna-Richards/e/B002BOBPE8/

Colleen Hoover

Introduction

New York Times bestselling YA romance novelist Colleen Hoover published her debut novel, "Slammed", in January 2012, closely followed by its sequel "Point of Retreat". Both novels have been hugely popular, garnering praise such as "a heart-wrenching, emotional, yet somehow humorous journey of two souls that are destined to be together, despite the factors that stand in their way".

The Interview

Tell us about yourself and your background?

I have always loved to write, but have never thought about pursuing it as a career. I mostly wrote for fun in my spare time. I graduated with a degree in Social Work, got married and had children. I'm 32 now and have probably taken a good ten year break from writing while focusing on everything else.

I originally started writing SLAMMED because my 8 year old was in a community theatre play. During his nightly practices, I would read while sitting in the auditorium. I had recently been on a "slam poetry" kick on YouTube, so I thought it would be interesting to read a novel that included the art form. I

GENRE
YA Romance

searched online for a novel where the characters SLAMMED, but couldn't find one. The next night I brought my laptop to his practice and started writing. It was around December 1st and I thought maybe I could write a short-story and give it to my mother for Christmas. Little did I know I would be quickly consumed by the story-line and the characters. I worked eleven hour days at the time and would write as soon as I got home from work until I couldn't keep my eyes open. I wrote constantly, barely sleeping, for the entire month of December. As I wrote, I had my boss and my mother reading the chapters. They convinced me to try and publish it, but I didn't have the first clue as to how to go about doing it.

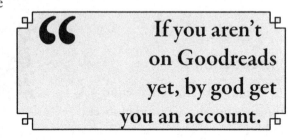

> If you aren't on Goodreads yet, by god get you an account.

What made you decide to self-publish?

I finished the manuscript Christmas Day and began editing while also researching publishing. I read about how hard it was to get published and came across an article about Amazon's self-publishing options. I didn't have a lot of faith in my story since it was my first attempt, so I chose to self-publish and uploaded the document in January. I chose to go with KDP Select at the time so that I could offer it for free to my friends and family, since I assumed they would be the only ones reading the book. I made it free the first few days and had about 4,000 free downloads. I was blown away the first month, sometimes selling between five and ten copies a day. I know that isn't a whole lot, but for a first time author who didn't expect anyone to read it, I was very happy.

How long have you been self-publishing?

I uploaded SLAMMED January 1st of this year. I'm pretty new at this, just about six months in. After publishing SLAMMED, I immediately started on the follow-up novel, POINT OF RETREAT, and uploaded it at the end of February.

What has been the most effective thing that you have done to promote your book?

I think KDP select played a big part in getting the word out. There aren't many avenues for self-published authors to effectively market, so being able to get the book into the hands of that many readers is a great opportunity.

I honestly don't do a lot to promote my book. I feel like Twitter and Facebook are only there for when you've already procured your readers. No one likes to see an author begging them to buy their work. I think it's more of a turn off to readers, especially if they've never heard of you. So the best thing I think that worked for me was developing the relationships with the people who have already read my book. Word of mouth is the biggest avenue to gain sales, and if you interact and respond to your fans, they'll get the word out. I love my readers and do my best to respond to every single email and message I receive. If they can take the time to tell me how much my book meant to them, I can take the time to thank them.

Do you do anything that you consider out of the ordinary to make your book a success?

The fact that both of my books became bestsellers within 90 days of being published is still astounding to me. I'm not going to sit here and say, "Yes, I expected this." Because I absolutely didn't expect this. I wrote these books because I love to write and was hoping to entertain a few friends and family. I think if I had any expectations that so many people would be reading them, it would have scared me too much to even finish them.

How have you gone about getting the word out about your book?

At this point, it's strictly word of mouth. Back in January when the book was free for a few days, my sisters bombarded everyone they knew to download it. I also include lyrics from my favorite band in the book. Their record company gave me permission to use lyrics as chapter headings. When the book was free one of the fan clubs wrote up an article about the book which also helped gain sales.

What has been your most successful self-published book, and how many have you sold?

Both of my books are almost equally successful. I haven't added up how many I've sold since they were published, but to give you an idea, SLAMMED has sold 12,000 copies in the last 21 days. POINT OF RETREAT has sold almost 10,000. These are only Amazon e-book sales. I also have my book on Barnes and Noble, as well as paperbacks.

What are your top tips for new indie authors?

I think KDP select is great for the first ninety days. After that, depending on an author's sales, they can opt out.

A good network of authors is great to have. I have made friends with several authors both in and out of my genre. I honestly feel the relationships I've made along the way have kept me sane.

I know this seems like a silly point, but you'd be surprised how many authors badmouth their bad reviews. It only comes back to bite them. You WILL get bad reviews. Not everyone is going to like your book. Some people will hate it. That's okay. The important thing is to (if you read the bad reviews) take what constructive criticism you can get. I've been known to read a comment from a bad review, agree with it and immediately go make edits. Being self-published, you lack the resources traditional publishers offer. Sometimes negative comments can be a huge source of constructive feedback.

Like I mentioned earlier, don't shove your book down people's throats. I was guilty of this right out of the gate and quickly realized it was more than likely hurting my sales, rather than helping them. Be patient.

GOODREADS! If you aren't on Goodreads yet, by god get you an account. Goodreads is like Facebook on crack for readers. I didn't know about it until a couple of months in. When someone reads your books, it shows up in all their Goodreads newsfeeds. Their reviews show up, their comments about your book. It's the absolute best free marketing there is.

And again...patience. It will take a while for things to pick up if you've got a good book. Do not compare your sales and experience to that of other authors. There are authors who have had tremendous luck and other authors who have had absolutely no luck. If you compare your rate of success to others, you will be disappointed. I have had a lot of luck in this industry and I don't take it for granted for a second. However, I would hate for other authors to expect to have a similar experience as me, then give up when that doesn't happen. Success comes to each person individually in different ways.

What do you think about the future of the publishing world?

I don't feel as though I've been in this industry long enough to offer an informative opinion. I do feel as though my manuscript would be sitting in a drawer if it weren't for the self-publishing boom. I'm not even going to say I'll never try to get a manuscript traditionally published. I believe each industry has its own perks and drawbacks and authors should research which works best for them. Although, I'd love to see a day where we no longer refer to things as "Traditionally-Published" "Indie" and "Self-published." It will be a great day when segregation of the publishing worlds happen and we can just refer to books by their genres alone. There has been and probably will be a negative stigma associated with self-publishing for a while to come. The only thing I can hope is that those that do self-publish put work out there that will continue to dispel the stigma.

Author Websites

http://www.colleenhoover.com/

Link to the Author's Amazon Author page

http://www.amazon.com/Colleen-Hoover/e/B006SKAK42/

Barbara Freethy

Introduction

New York Times bestselling romance author Barbara Freethy sold an astounding 2.2 million self-published titles in just 18 months by publishing her backlist, as well as new novels. Barbara has now published thirty novels, including The Wish Series and the Angel's Bay series.

The Interview

Tell us about yourself and your background?

I have a degree in Communication Studies from UC Santa Barbara. I worked in public relations for several years before deciding to write a novel. I sold my first book to Silhouette Romance and since then have sold books to Avon, NAL, and Pocket Books. I have self-published two original books, A SECRET WISH and JUST A WISH AWAY. I now have 30 published titles and many of my books have appeared on the USA Today and New York Times Bestseller List including one title, SUMMER SECRETS, that hit #1 on the New York Times.

GENRE
Romantic Suspense

What made you decide to self-publish?

I started self-publishing with some of the backlist titles – books for which the rights had reverted to me after they went out of print. I then moved on to self-publishing original work.

How long have you been self-publishing?

I started self-publishing in January 2011 and by June of 2012, I had sold over 2.2 million units of my self-published titles.

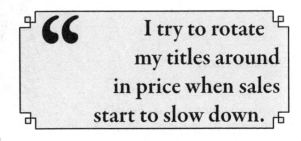

What has been the most effective thing that you have done to promote your book?

There's no one thing I can point to as the "thing to do" but rather a cumulative effort on a lot of different fronts. I have multiple titles to work with, which is a big advantage. I have given some books away for free, which helped entice new readers my way. I have used sales promotions at 99 cents for short periods of time. I participate on all of the social media platforms, and I write a lot!

Do you do anything that you consider out of the ordinary to make your book a success?

I stay very focused on my sales numbers and I try to rotate my titles around in price when sales start to slow down. I've changed covers and have seen improved results. I've played with covers until I found a look that would become my brand.

How have you gone about getting the word out about your book?

Through social media and newsletters to people who have written to me about my books.

What has been your most successful self-published book, and how many have you sold?

Summer Secrets hit #1 on Amazon and #1 on the NYT and was also in the top ten on B&N. To be honest, I don't have the exact sales figures for each of my titles. I'm not a spreadsheet type of person, as I'm usually in the midst of writing a book. But I would estimate that book had sold over 300,000 copies.

What are your top tips for new indie authors?

Write more than one book! It's much easier to sell books when you have one that you can offer for free or at a cheaper price and then readers come back to buy the second book. Plus, readers who love your work will want more books! So once you're done with one project, move immediately on to the next.

Make sure you participate in social media but don't go crazy with it. 30 minutes a day can be very effective.

Be ready to make changes... you can change covers, you can change your description and you can select better keywords. Find what works for you.

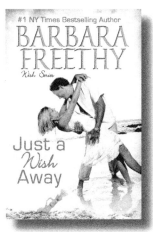

What do you think about the future of the publishing world?

I'm very excited about publishing. There are more opportunities for writers than ever before. There are certainly more ways to bring your book to life and it's a wonderful time to be writing a book!

Author Websites

http://www.barbarafreethy.com/

Link to the Author's Amazon Author page

www.amazon.com/Barbara-Freethy/e/B00II9OPSK/

Joseph Lallo

Introduction

Fantasy and science fiction author Joseph Lallo has been publishing since January 2010 and has released six books, including the highly popular Book of Deacon Trilogy. He loves interacting with fans and publishes fan artwork on his website.

The Interview

Tell us about yourself and your background?

I was born and raised in Bayonne, NJ. It is a small and relatively unremarkable town a few minutes away from New York City. I am the youngest of three brothers, and the son of a stay at home mom and a dad who did anything and everything necessary to keep the family fed. (That includes factory work, butchery, and train inspection.) Though I'd always had an interest in reading and writing, I'd never intended it as a career. I actually went to college for Computer Engineering, and left with a Master's Degree in the subject. Since just before graduation, I've been working in IT. The success of the books has been a relatively recent and very welcome development.

GENRE
Fantasy / Science Fiction

What made you decide to self-publish?

After spending a spectacular amount of spare time (as well as a fair amount of time that I technically couldn't spare) writing a book, I felt as though the only way to justify the effort was to try to have it published. I did some research and found that the proper way to go about it was to seek out a literary agent. Once I'd selected a few dozen that seemed to represent my genre and didn't appear to be scam artists, I started writing query letters. A year later I had about two dozen rejection letters, mostly form letters, and a pile of agents who never got back to me. I was willing to let it go, but the handful of friends who had read my book pushed me to give self-publishing a try. Boy, am I glad I listened to them.

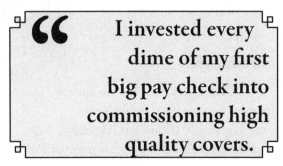

I invested every dime of my first big pay check into commissioning high quality covers.

How long have you been self-publishing?

My first book was self-published in January 2010, and I've been releasing a title or two per year since then.

What has been the most effective thing that you have done to promote your book?

Without a doubt, the most effective bit of promotion I've done was writing a series and pricing the first book as low as possible. The e-book of The Book of Deacon is free.

Do you do anything that you consider out of the ordinary to make your book a success?

Aside from giving one of my books away? I continually reinvest into the books. When I first started to earn money from my books, I invested every dime of my first big pay check into commissioning high quality covers. (I highly recommend it, by the way. It tripled my sales.) I then took that money and hired a professional editor to clean up my grammar. I'm perpetually trying to hunt down and correct any lingering errors in my books, and I try to improve anywhere they seem to be lacking. (Excluding the actual plot and story. I feel as though changing that would be unfair to readers who had read the original story.)

How have you gone about getting the word out about your book?

Most of my efforts to spread the word about my books have been devoted to making myself as available to my readers as possible. Early on, I responded to as many customer reviews as I could. As interest began to pick up, I created a website and distributed my contact info in the back of my e-books. I continue to reply to every email, tweet, and comment I get, and I try to

listen to any requests that come from the fans. This has led to starting a forum, helping to produce an official wiki, starting a Facebook fan page, and even setting up a way for readers to purchase an autographed copy of the paperback. I make sure to spread the word whenever anyone does something related to my books, whether it is a review, a piece of fan art, or even just a blog mention. I feel that word of mouth is the best way to spread the word. I just help it along.

What has been your most successful self-published book, and how many have you sold?

That depends upon how you define successful. Obviously my free book has gotten the most exposure, but hasn't made me very much money. I don't keep up-to-date numbers on my overall book sales, but I can tell you my numbers for Amazon. The Book of Deacon, in is free e-book form, has been downloaded over 110,000 times. The most profitable book is the second book in the trilogy, The Great Convergence. The e-book has been purchased over 13,000 times.

What are your top tips for new indie authors?

There are three things I would recommend for people just getting started as indie authors. First, make sure you have done your very best to format and proofread your book. Professional editing isn't strictly necessary, but you should get a few different sets of eyes to scan for errors. My own books lost a few stars early on due to the copious errors that made it into the first edition. Second, take the time to make a professional-looking cover. I cannot tell you the difference a well made cover has made. It doesn't have to be a masterpiece, but there are a lot of people out there who won't give a second look to a book that has a cover that looks homemade, so consider getting a professional if that's beyond your ability. Finally, talk to your fans. It is fun, it helps spread the word, and they appreciate it.

What do you think about the future of the publishing world?

I think that there will always be a place for traditionally published paperback and hard cover books, but the focus of the literary world is certainly expanding. Traditional publishers are beginning to lose their grip on the publishing industry as the resources to publish and publicize your own books are becoming more and more available. Between e-books and Print-On-Demand, do-it-yourself authors are able to provide a similar level of convenience and quality to the consumer in terms of format and availability. As a result, it just comes down to quality of writing to make the decision of who succeeds and who fails, and it is the reader rather than the publisher who gets to make the decision. Many would call this a change for the better. I'm a bit biased, as you might imagine, but I'm inclined to agree.

Any other thoughts you would like to share?

For people who are thinking of taking the leap and putting their hard work out there, through either the traditional or self-publishing route, please remember to be patient and persistent. It took more than a year for my books to get their first reviews, and months more before I'd earned enough to receive a payment. You may not be an overnight success, but there is always hope for the next day.

Author Websites

http://www.bookofdeacon.com/

Link to the Author's Amazon Author page

http://www.amazon.com/Joseph-Lallo/e/B004K9UEP8/

Rebecca Forster

Introduction

New York Times bestselling thriller writer Rebecca Forster was an established author when she decided to self-publish "Before Her Eyes" in 2010, which quickly became a bestseller. She is known for her Witness Series of legal thrillers and regularly speaks to writers' groups, as well as teaching at the UCLA Writers Program and with The Young Writers Conference.

The Interview

Tell us about yourself and your background?

I started writing on a crazy dare and then spent the next 25 years publishing novels in New York. They ranged from women's fiction to thrillers. When Keeping Counsel hit the USA Today Bestseller list I found my literary home. I have written over 25 books, have two screenplays in development and continue to add to the witness series every year. The witness series has been on Amazons top 100 legal thrillers for over five months at this writing, four of them consistently in the top 10.

Before writing, I was in advertising/marketing both in San Francisco and Los Angeles. I hold a BA in English and an MBA.

GENRE
Legal Thriller

I have been married to my husband, a superior court judge, for thirty-six years and have two grown sons: one is in film and the other is a playwright. I love traveling and have been all over the world, play tennis and sew and quilt in my spare time.

What made you decide to self-publish?

New York was tightening up, the publishing world was changing. I saw a chance to truly direct my own career as well as to branch out creatively. Before Her Eyes, one of my favorite books, never caught the imagination of a New York publisher and yet it has been on Amazon's police procedural, thriller, and teen fantasy bestseller lists.

> **"** The digital world moves so fast that if you don't have the next book for people to read they will turn to another author who does.

How long have you been self-publishing?

Two years, although I traditionally published for twenty-five.

What has been the most effective thing that you have done to promote your book?

The most effective strategy has been offering the first book in my series free.

Do you do anything that you consider out of the ordinary to make your book a success?

This may not be out of the ordinary but I remind myself every day to take every word I write very seriously. Whether it's words used to create a book or words used to answer an email, I try to make sure they are the right ones. In the first instance it is because I want to entertain readers in the best way possible, and in the second instance I want to communicate how personally I take every message some one sends me. I have had some pen pals for 25 years. That proves words are important.

How have you gone about getting the word out about your book?

I was lucky that I already had some name recognition. However, the indie universe is huge, so I engage in all the accepted promotional activity: Twitter, Linked In, and Facebook. I also do some limited advertising. Mostly, I hope my work speaks for itself. I believe word of mouth has always been the best form of promotion.

What has been your most successful self-published book, and how many have you sold?

The witness series has been awfully successful and accounts for about 90% of my sales. I republished the first three as an indie and the fourth, Expert Witness, was written specifically for digital, came out in 2012. Before Her Eyes was also specifically written for the indie market also. I spent the first year of my indie

career simply getting things in order. I count November 2011 as the real beginning of my efforts as an indie. In the first six months I sold over 100,000 copies of all my books.

What are your top tips for new indie authors?

Before you begin promoting make sure you have at least three books published. They don't have to be a series even though series are very popular. The digital world moves so fast that if you don't have the next book for people to read they will turn to another author who does.

What do you think about the future of the publishing world?

My best guess? Digital is here to stay, print books will be POD, and independent bookstores with specific points of view will start cropping up all over. I don't think we'll be seeing the huge distributions of print titles that we have seen in the past. Brick and mortar stores are contracting space so there isn't room for the physical product any longer.

Any other thoughts you would like to share?

Love what you do, share what you know, always be open to dialogue with those who write and those who read.

Author Websites

http://www.rebeccaforster.com/

Link to the Author's Amazon Author page

http://www.amazon.com/Rebecca-Forster/e/B001HCZP3W/

Caryn Moya Block

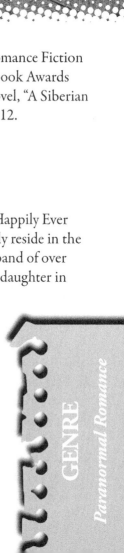

Introduction

Caryn Moya Block is a new indie author, having self-published her first novel in January 2012. Just six months later, she was named as a finalist in the Romance Fiction – Contemporary category of the 2012 Global E-book Awards for her debut novel "Alpha's Mate". Her second novel, "A Siberian Werewolf in London", was published in March 2012.

The Interview

Tell us about yourself and your background?

I love romantic movies and stories that end "Happily Ever After." I'm an avid reader and writer and I currently reside in the Virginia Piedmont. My "pack" consist of my husband of over thirty years, my two grown sons and my beautiful daughter in law, one cat, one turtle, and four Shetland Sheepdogs. I suffer from "Multiple Sheltie Syndrome", because one is never enough. I've been intrigued with the paranormal since seeing my first ghost at three years of age.

What made you decide to self-publish?

I wanted to get my stories out to the public. I had been watching the publishing industry change and thought I would give it a try.

GENRE *Paranormal Romance*

How long have you been self-publishing?

My first book was released on January 1, 2012.

What has been the most effective thing that you have done to promote your book?

Social Media and Marketing. I try to be in contact with my readers on a daily basis.

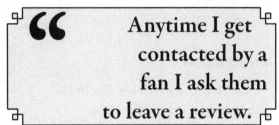
" Anytime I get contacted by a fan I ask them to leave a review.

Do you do anything that you consider out of the ordinary to make your book a success?

I watch other authors to see what they are doing.

How have you gone about getting the word out about your book?

I tell everyone I know and then anytime I get contacted by a fan I ask them to leave a review and help spread the word.

What has been your most successful self-published book, and how many have you sold?

My first book, "Alpha's Mate", sold over 17,000 copies in its first 4 months.

What are your top tips for new indie authors?

Read all the fine print on the sites you are considering to upload to. There may be hidden fees or fees paid annually. I actually did not have a problem with the sites I chose to use. But there are some out there that will charge you an upfront fee and then tack on an annual fee per book. For those of us selling our books for 99 cents it did not seem like a good choice to me. I would suggest to all authors, ask around and see what sites their friends are using. But don't forget to read the fine print or you might have some surprises in the future.

What do you think about the future of the publishing world?

I believe e-publishing will become the norm and the readers themselves will decide whether a book is enjoyable or not.

Any other thoughts you would like to share?

This has been an amazing journey for me. Don't be afraid to reach for success.

Author Websites

http://carynmoyablock.com/
https://www.facebook.com/#!/CarynMoyaBlock
https://twitter.com/#!/CarynMoyaBlock

Link to the Author's Amazon Author page

http://www.amazon.com/Caryn-Moya-Block/e/B006U3O3V8/

Denise Grover Swank

Introduction

Bestselling, full-time author Denise Grover Swank has published eight books since July 2011, with another three to be released this year. Her books include the awarding winning The Chosen Series, the On the Other Side Series and her two Rose Gardner mysteries.

The Interview

Tell us about yourself and your background?

I'm a widow and the mother of six kids, but only five live at home. I've always written and tried to write a novel several times, never finishing. My past careers have been in medical lab, and after I went back to school to get an interior design degree, a kitchen and bath designer. In the fall of 2009, I found out about NaNoWriMo and decided I was either going to write a novel or stop talking about it. On November 30, I had 69,000 words and I finished my novel on December 10. When I typed the words "The End", I finally realized what I wanted to be when I grew up. Since that first - unpublished - novel, I've written and published six more. I'm currently a full time author.

GENRE
Romance/YA Paranormal

What made you decide to self-publish?

I'd written and sent off three books in three completely different genres, getting some replies and some near misses with agents on two of the books. But no one seemed interested in my rom com mystery, Twenty-Eight and a Half Wishes. At the same time, I'd been paying attention to the self-publishing world and noticed that the stigma was easing. I decided I loved my book Twenty-Eight too much to let it die so I self-published it in July, 2011. I hoped to sell 1000 copies by the end of the year - my pie in the sky goal. I sold 1000 copies by September and cried like a baby. I'd achieved my goal for success.

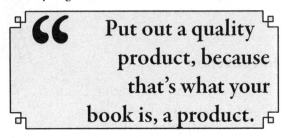

Put out a quality product, because that's what your book is, a product.

My new goal was to sell 10,000 total books by the end of the year. At midnight December 31, I'd published three more books and sold over 26,000 copies. I've now published two more books and two short stories. I sold my 100,000th book on May 29, 2011, slightly less than eleven months after I published my first book.

How long have you been self-publishing?

One year. I released my first book in July 2011.

What has been the most effective thing that you have done to promote your book?

The thing about marketing in self-publishing is that it's always changing. I got my initial start and success with book review blog tours. I ran Chosen through two book tours, back to back, and that is what propelled it to #1 in Contemporary Fantasy in December, 2011 and into the Top 100 of the Kindle

Store. I released Hunted, the second book in the series, at the end of November and it climbed into the Top 5 of Contemporary Fantasy and was #1 in Hot New Releases for both Romantic Suspense and Contemporary Fantasy. I received an offer from a Turkish publisher.

Around that time, Amazon introduced Select and I reluctantly joined when I saw my rankings start to slip. It was no wonder they fell before I enrolled. I signed up December 18 and had over 700 borrows by the end of the month on Chosen alone.

I decided to try my first free promo for Chosen the first week of February, 2012. I notified all the big sites as well as some smaller ones that it would be free. I was completely unprepared for the success of the promo. Chosen was #2 in the Free Kindle store and had over 36,000 free downloads in two days. After it went back to regular price, it was #2 in Movers and Shakers, spent ten days in the Top 100 of the Kindle store and climbed to #19. It was #1 in all Science Fiction and Fantasy. I sold 11,000 copies in three weeks. Chosen has spent over 180 days in the Top 100 of Science Fiction and Fantasy. I received an offer of representation from my agent, Amanda Luedeke of MacGregor Literary.

I ran Chosen as another free promo the first week of May. The results weren't as good as the first promo, but I didn't expect them to be. Still, Chosen climbed back into the 100 rankings and the sales of the other two books in the series increased. I attracted the attention of a major movie studio and we are currently in discussions about making Chosen into a feature film. To date, I've sold over 85,000 books in the series. Other authors have sold many, many more books, but I'm not complaining about my results.

I've also had very good, very short term success with Pixel of Ink features. I've had little success with other paid ads. I've taken out coop ads in RT Book Review but found little benefit other than the starred review they give. I've seen no increase in sales.

Do you do anything that you consider out of the ordinary to make your book a success?

I make sure my books are attention getting and the pacing is tight as well as being well written. My readers say they can't put my books down. One of my favorite reviews is a two star review of Chosen that said "Strange book, but I couldn't stop reading it." I call that a win.

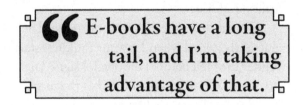

I'm a business woman who writes books. I came into this awareness in December, 2011 when Chosen and Hunted were selling well. I realized that I could make a living doing this and I needed to get my act together. I wrote a twenty-three page business plan, formed a business - Bramagioia Enterprises. My entire focus changed and I've done very well. Again, many others have done better than I have, but I'm quite happy with my five-figure monthly Amazon checks.

I don't have a magic pill or secret formula. I have no idea why some books sell better than others. I thought my rom com mystery series would sell just as well as The Chosen series, but it doesn't despite its very strong, positive reviews. I think we can promo in many different ways, but at least a small portion of any book's success is luck.

How have you gone about getting the word out about your book?

I sign my books up for book review blog tours. Twenty-Nine and a Half Reasons, the second book in my rom com mystery series, comes out the end of June 2012 and I've signed it up for three blog tours as well as gotten some bigger sites to review it soon after its release. I do guest posts and interviews. Sometimes it's not even about selling a book, sometimes it's about getting your name out in front of readers so that they begin to see it and say "Oh! I've heard of her." That reader might not buy one of my books for another two years, but I'm in this for the long haul. E-books have a long tail, and I'm taking advantage of that.

What has been your most successful self-published book, and how many have you sold?

Chosen is my most successful book. I've sold over 43,000 copies.

What are your top tips for new indie authors?

Put out a quality product, because that's what your book is, a product. You want your reader to say "That book was self-published? I had no idea." When you're first starting out you often don't have much money and you're wondering if you should sink money into something that might not sell. The reality is 80% of all books will sell less than 200 copies.

Here's what you cannot live without: a good copy editor and a good cover. Have friends with an English degree or self-proclaimed grammar Nazis proofread your manuscript. Find really tough, critical beta readers to critique your story development. But do not consider pressing Publish without a professional copy editor.

Some books take time to catch on with readers. Your book might only have 50 sales for a few months, then suddenly alien cow stories are hot, and low and behold, your book is an alien cow story! It's not uncommon for self-published books in the Top 100 in the Kindle store to be several months, to a year or more old. That's the true beauty of self-publishing. There is no limited amount of time to prove your book's worth.

What do you think about the future of the publishing world?

I see traditional publishers continuing to struggle, but I also see them using the self-published author pool as the new slush pile. We've already seen it with Amanda Hocking, EL James and

Tracy Garvis-Graves. We're going to see this more and more.

I do think that the self-published book world will become more and more competitive within itself. More Indie authors are publishing, now more than ever, and that's a lot of hands waving in the air shouting "Notice me!" I think already established, successful indie authors will have an advantage since they will already have a reader base.

I think one the best sales tools for the self-published author is that traditionally published books tend to have outrageously high e-book prices. My fifteen year old daughter is a voracious reader and I gave her a Kindle Fire for Christmas. I've studied her reading and buying habits. It was a novelty to her in the beginning, and she much preferred print books. But sometime in March, she realized she could download a book onto her Kindle and she didn't have to wait for me to take her to Barnes & Noble or the ordered print book from Amazon. She could read it immediately. With unlimited access to new books, she soon realized that the monthly book allowance I give her was getting used up with $9.99 e-books. Now she actively searches out indie published books. She rarely spends more than $3.99 for a book, occasionally spending $4.99, but then reluctantly. She reads the Look Inside and decides if it's something she's interested in or if the writing is good. She also runs a YA book review blog and often reviews the books she reads.

My biggest worry at this point is that the Big 6 will come to their senses and lower their e-book prices, making them more competitive with Indie books. THIS is another reason you want to produce a quality book, because if it's your poorly edited book with a bad cover, up against a Big 6 book (which doesn't necessarily mean it will have a great cover), which one do you think the reader is going to pick?

Any other thoughts you would like to share?

This is truly an exciting time in publishing! I can't wait to see what happens next!

Author Websites

http://www.denisegroverswank.com/

Link to the Author's Amazon Author page

http://www.amazon.com/Denise-Grover-Swank/e/B005ANAB6K/

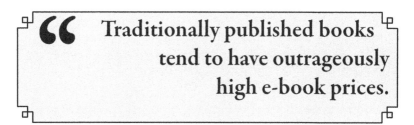

" Traditionally published books tend to have outrageously high e-book prices.

Mainak Dhar

Introduction

Indian author Mainak Dhar combines self-publishing e-books on Amazon with traditionally publishing paperbacks in India. He has enjoyed huge success with his indie publishing career, with Alice in Deadland being downloaded nearly 70,000 times in the first six months after release.

The Interview

Tell us about yourself and your background?

I describe myself as a cubicle dweller by day and writer by night, but my dream of being a writer is something I've had for as long as I can remember. My first 'published' work was in Grade 7 when I stapled together my poems and solutions to the Maths textbook and sold them to my classmates, earning a profit of $12.50 that was promptly spent on ice cream and comics. Stephen King once said that the moment someone pays you a cent for your writing, you're a professional writer, and in my mind, that was when my career as a writer began.

GENRE
Horror / Science Fiction

What made you decide to self-publish?

I had been traditionally published in India for some years, with novels published by majors like Random House and Penguin. However, I was not really able to reach international readers with any scale. When I discovered Kindle Direct Publishing and the opportunity and platform it gave to writers to reach readers globally, I first put up a couple of books from my backlist - Line of Control, Heroes R Us and Vimana. As I understood just how great an opportunity this was to reach readers, I began writing novels that were uploaded first to Amazon, without even approaching publishers. In the last 12 months, I have written three totally original novels that were self-published on Amazon- Zombiestan, Alice in Deadland and Through The Killing Glass: Alice in Deadland Book II. Subsequently, all three have been picked up for India paperback rights by a major publisher, and in a way my writing journey has come full circle. It has also opened up a lot of new opportunities - I've been approached for foreign language rights and have secured an audiobook deal.

> I try and reinvest about 20% of my royalties every month into advertising and sponsorships to keep building awareness.

How long have you been self-publishing?

My first books were uploaded in the last few days of February 2011. So I've completed just over one year.

What has been the most effective thing that you have done to promote your book?

Write the next one.

Do you do anything that you consider out of the ordinary to make your book a success and what are your top tips for new indie authors?

I don't think success in any business is rocket science - all it requires is getting some fundamentals right. What's difficult is being able to get them right consistently. The basics I focus on are - first and foremost, writing the best story I can. Second, invest in a professional cover design. That is simply defined as a cover which when put next to the bestselling books by the biggest name authors and publishers in your genre would still be competitive and compelling. Third, get my work professionally edited. Fourth, get the right value. When I began self-publishing, I priced all my work at 99 cents, since I wanted to totally remove any barriers that readers may have had in trying an unknown author. As I've built more of a reader base, I am now pricing my work more consistently at $2.99, and last month, I sold as many books at $2.99 as I did at 99 cents.

The other, and really important thing is to build a portfolio of work ('write the next book' is not just a glib cliché). Having more work out there helps you build a reader base, helps you increase chances of being discovered and indeed, you can then deliberately start using your portfolio (eg. Putting blurbs/ excerpts of one book at the back of another etc).

How have you gone about getting the word out about your book?

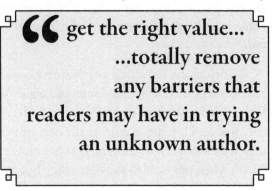

> get the right value... ...totally remove any barriers that readers may have in trying an unknown author.

I do book sponsorships on blogs like Kindle Nation Daily and the Kindle Fire Department but not much more than that. I have a full time day job and a family, and I try and focus my writing time on actually writing - not doing too many fancy promotional things. So I try and keep the promotional part on as much of an auto-pilot as possible- book a bunch of slots for the next few months and then forget about it, and focus on writing. More than focusing on short term payout, I try and reinvest about 20% of my royalties every month into advertising and sponsorships to keep building awareness. I think that's true for any business - if you want to make money from day 1, chances are you'll be disappointed. Invest for the long term and you'll be surprised at how momentum builds. In my first month, I sold only 118 books, and I did not 'break even' for the first six months - now I've recovered all that initial investment in design, editing and advertising many, many times over.

The other thing I do is to try and leverage every connection with readers. Every time I get a mail from a reader, I ensure I reply within the day with a personalized note v/s a form letter. The one thing I have done on social media is to create a Facebook group for Alice in Deadland. It does not have a huge number of members, but it's great fun to interact with readers and also that has become a great source of ideas - I run polls on future ideas, bounce of plotlines - and it makes the writing and reading experience more interactive than being a one way street.

What has been your most successful self-published book, and how many have you sold?

My biggest success till date in terms of copies sold has been Alice in Deadland - which has had close to 70,000 paid downloads (sales+borrows) in its first six months. I just uploaded its sequel Through The Killing Glass, and it's had a good start as well, with almost 2000 paid downloads in its first full month - and priced at $2.99 v/s Alice in Deadland at 99 cents. Vimana has had close to 25,000 sales, and two other titles, Line of Control and Zombiestan should hit the 10,000 mark in the next couple of months. I am now working on the third book in the Alice in Deadland trilogy, which is meant to be a prequel.

What do you think about the future of the publishing world?

It's an exciting time to be a writer, and the way we can reach readers has changed so much in the last few years that it's almost unrecognizable. Having been traditionally published as well as having self-published, the one thing that I do sometimes cringe at is the 'ghetto mentality' on both sides, with many publishers and traditionally published writers looking down at indies and some indie writers regarding traditional publishing as some sort of evil empire. I would say to any aspiring author, write a damn good book and know who your readers are. Once that is done, then pick whichever route best helps you reach those readers- that's the best, and most pragmatic approach to take in a dynamic industry like this v/s forming rigid opinions on indie v/s traditional publishing. In my case, for the Indian market, traditional publishing still make sense given low e-book penetration so I have a dual business model - self-pub on KDP for global audiences and sell paperback rights to traditional publishers in India. As the Indian market evolves, I may well change that stand. So, be flexible, have an open mind and embrace change. That is the best way to stay on top of an industry like this.

Author Websites

http://www.mainakdhar.com/

Link to the Author's Amazon Author page

http://www.amazon.com/Mainak-Dhar/e/B001IOBOTI/

Imogen Rose

Introduction

YA paranormal romance author Imogen Rose's story is one of accidental self-publishing, but she is now a bestselling full-time author. Her books include the popular Portal Chronicles series and the Bonfire Chronicles series.

The Interview

Tell us about yourself and your background.

My background is in science, with a PhD in Immunology. Born in Sweden, I moved to London in my twenties, and now live in New Jersey. I stumbled into writing accidentally when I found the "publish" button on CreateSpace, where I had made my way to get a story bound for my daughter. That story turned into the Portal Chronicles, my bestselling YA time travel romance.

What made you decide to self-publish?

I stumbled into it purely by accident.

How long have you been self-publishing?

I published my first novel in 2010.

GENRE: YA Paranormal

What has been the most effective thing that you have done to promote your book?

I try everything, and I have learned to be very flexible. What worked three years ago does not necessarily work today.

Do you do anything that you consider out of the ordinary to make your book a success?

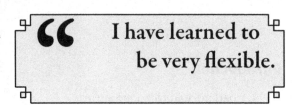

No, not really.

How have you gone about getting the word out about your book?

I have an amazing bunch of loyal fans. In addition, a large number of book bloggers have shown their support by giving me opportunities to advertise my books on their sites.

What has been your most successful self-published book, and how many have you sold?

I don't share my numbers, but my most successful book to date is Portal (Portal Chronicles Book One).

What are your top tips for new indie authors?

Put out a well-edited book with a nice cover, and then do everything in your power to market it.

What do you think about the future of the publishing world?

It's hard to say. Every day brings news of innovations in publishing. I think it's a great time for indie authors as long as we are flexible and make sure that our work is good.

Author Websites

http://www.imogenrose.com/

Link to the Author's Amazon Author page

http://www.amazon.com/Imogen-Rose/e/B0035Z3ZPO/

CJ Lyons

Introduction

New York Times bestselling author CJ Lyons' 'thrillers with heart' have been published to critical acclaim and have won many awards. CJ's books include the Lucy Guardino FBI thrillers, the Hart and Drake series, Angels of Mercy series, Shadow Ops series, standalone thrillers, a new series co-written with Erin Brockovich, and her non-fiction guide to writing a novel "No Rules Just Write: Crafting the Character Driven Novel".

Former ER doctor CJ knows just what it takes to be a successful author and she blogs, gives advice, shares tools and resources, and offers a course on indie publishing over at her No Rules Just Write website - http://www.norulesjustwrite.com The Interview

Tell us about yourself and your background?

I was a Pediatric ER doctor for 17 years before leaving to write full time. Now I am a New York Times and USA Today Bestseller. Both careers were adrenalin-rush of roller coaster rides!

GENRE Thriller

What made you decide to self-publish?

My fans wanted my books available faster than my NYC publisher was publishing them, so I first began self-publishing as a marketing tool. It was a way to get my books into the hands of my readers faster.

> **I use a Street Team of ~150 fans and give them advanced readers copies.**

How long have you been self-publishing?

Since Nov, 2009

What has been the most effective thing that you have done to promote your book?

Giving away books.

Do you do anything that you consider out of the ordinary to make your book a success?

I use a Street Team of ~150 fans and give them advanced copies so that they're ready with reviews on the day a new book is released.

How have you gone about getting the word out about your book?

My monthly newsletter, Facebook page, website.

What has been your most successful self-published book, and how many have you sold?

BLIND FAITH sold 250,000+ copies so far

What are your top tips for new indie authors?

Don't get caught up in the promotion whirlwind, your best promotional tool is writing the next book. The more books out there the more your fans will do the promotional work for you.

What do you think about the future of the publishing world?

This is a renaissance for writers. For the first time we can not only make a living wage but engage our readers in a way that traditional publishers can't. I believe the future lies in publishers doing what they do best: creating keepsake print books and distributing them; agents selling subrights; authors writing their best books possible; and readers reaping the rewards.

Any other thoughts you would like to share?

Here's the skinny on the Street Team…I originally used my self-published e-books as reader appreciation gifts for folks who signed up for my newsletter.

After giving away several hundred e-books I realized that readers wanted more free reads--and that one way to help new readers find my books was more reviews, so I offered free e-books

Top Tips from Successful Self-Published Authors

to folks who posted a review. A win/win for everyone. These select "uber fans" became my Street Team. When I realized how many folks enjoyed leaving reviews (and all I ask for is an honest review--sometimes they're five stars, occasionally they're three) I organized them into a separate mailing list.

I email them before each new book release, offering advance readers' copies so there will be reviews ready when the book comes out.

I also email them between books and give them free reads--sometimes physical books, sometimes ereads--as well as exclusive behind the scene bonuses, sneak peaks of new projects, and I've even done special book club visits for them and one Street Team member won the right to be a character in BLOOD STAINED.

I know of other writers who ask their Street Teams to literally hit the streets leaving bookmarks in bookstores or moving their books to the front of stores, but all I ask is the occasional tweet or FB post spreading the word and if they enjoy a book to take a few minutes to leave a review. I try to keep it painless and fun.

You can learn more about the Street Team Family here: http://cjlyons.net/for-readers/join-cjs-street-team/

Author Websites

http://cjlyons.net/
http://thrillerswithheart.com/
http://www.norulesjustwrite.com

Link to the Author's Amazon Author page

http://www.amazon.com/C.-J.-Lyons/e/B001JSJQ7K/

Bella Andre

Introduction

Bella Andre's latest romance, published in May 2012, was an instant worldwide bestseller, and her books have been featured in Cosmopolitan Magazine's Red Hot Reads, as well as appearing regularly on the bestseller lists. She is known for "sensual, empowered stories enveloped in heady romance" (Publisher's Weekly).

The Interview

Tell us about yourself and your background?

I've always been a writer - songs first and then non-fiction books. As soon as I started writing romance novels ten years ago I knew I'd found my career.

What made you decide to self-publish?

I've always been a ravenous romance reader - devouring a book a day when I can. One day, two characters started to have a conversation inside my head, and I decided to write it down. A couple of years later I sold my first novel. After writing for four major publishers, in 2010 I found myself with more stories to tell and the self-publishing revolution just beginning. I took a leap of faith and wrote the sequel to my most popular novel at the time, TAKE ME, which is about a full-figured heroine and the man she's loved forever. LOVE ME (the brother and sister's story) came out July 2010 and when readers kept writing to thank me for writing the love story they'd been waiting for, I wrote my next original self-published novel, GAME FOR LOVE, the 3rd book in my Bad Boys of Football series. I released it Christmas 2010 and was the first self-published author to hit a major top 25 bestseller list with my e-book. Since then, I have written and released 5 books in my Sullivan family contemporary romance series. The latest, IF YOU WERE MINE, came out in May 2012.

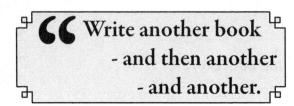

> Write another book - and then another - and another.

Thanks to self-publishing, when my fans ask for more books - and for them to come out quickly - I am able to give them exactly what they want!

How long have you been self-publishing?

Two years.

What has been the most effective thing that you have done to promote your book?

Write another book - and then another - and another. I also try to have a lot of personal contact with my readers via email, newsletters and social media.

Do you do anything that you consider out of the ordinary to make your book a success?

Honestly, I focused the bulk of my energies on writing the best book I can. I've found that when my books connect with my readers, the rest just falls into place.

How have you gone about getting the word out about your book?

I send out a newsletter with each new release and also use social media to let my readers know about each new book release.

What has been your most successful self-published book, and how many have you sold?

Each book seems to be more successful than the last, which is great. I ONLY HAVE EYES FOR YOU (The Sullivans #4) debuted as the #1 romance at Apple iBooks in the US, UK, Australia and Canada, was a top 10 bestseller at BN, and a top 10 romance bestseller at Amazon. I've sold 700,000 self-published e-books as of May 2012, the majority at an average price of $4.99.

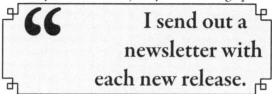

> " I send out a newsletter with each new release.

What are your top tips for new indie authors?

Besides writing a great book? Do your research, pay attention to the constant changes in publishing and e-books. And spend time making sure your cover is fantastic.

What do you think about the future of the publishing world?

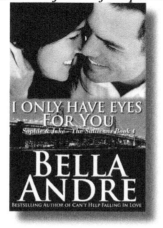

Top Tips from Successful Self-Published Authors

I think there's never been a better time to be a writer!

Author Websites

http://bellaandre.com/
http://Facebook.com/bellaandrefans
http://twitter.com/bellaandre

Link to the Author's Amazon Author page

www.amazon.com/Bella-Andre/e/B001JS38XI/

Theresa Ragan

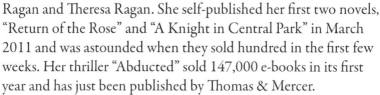

Introduction

Award-winning, bestselling author Theresa Ragan writes in a variety of genres and under two names: T.R. Ragan and Theresa Ragan. She self-published her first two novels, "Return of the Rose" and "A Knight in Central Park" in March 2011 and was astounded when they sold hundred in the first few weeks. Her thriller "Abducted" sold 147,000 e-books in its first year and has just been published by Thomas & Mercer.

The Interview

Tell us about yourself and your background?

I have been writing for nineteen years and have garnered six Golden Heart nominations in Romance Writers of America's Golden Heart Competition. I live with my husband, Joe, and the youngest of my four children in California. I am known for writing medieval time travels, romantic comedy, romantic suspense, and thrillers under the name T.R. Ragan. In a little over a year, I've sold 300,000 e-books. In March of 2012 I signed my first publishing contract with Thomas & Mercer, an Amazon imprint. Many people have told me that self-publishing is the end to a writer's career, but for me, it's just the beginning!

GENRE: Thriller

What made you decide to self-publish?

I was working full time as a Legal Secretary and pregnant with my fourth and last child when I read my first romance novel. I knew instantly that I wanted to be a writer. For the next 19 years I did everything I could to learn my craft. I wrote every day. I joined Romance Writers of America and I attended workshops and conferences all over the U.S. I joined critique groups and I drove hours every week to exchange pages with other writers. I entered the Golden Heart contest for unpublished writers because I had heard that a final in the Golden Heart was practically a guarantee into the publishing world. I finaled SIX times and yet I still did not sell a book. I signed with two agents and I worked with more than a few editors, but still no sale. Hundreds of rejections later, my youngest child was going off to college. The year was 2011. I heard other writers talking about self-publishing on Amazon and I knew that I had to try it. I had nothing to lose. I self-published my first two books, expecting to sell ten books and instead I sold hundreds. After a mention on Pixel of Ink, sales took off and I was selling thousands of books.

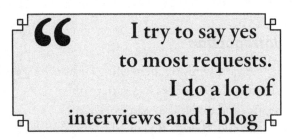

> **I try to say yes to most requests. I do a lot of interviews and I blog**

How long have you been self-publishing?

I released my first book in March of 2011.

What has been the most effective thing that you have done to promote your book?

The best thing I did was spend the first three months promoting my books and myself. Everything I did in the beginning was free. I made my own website using blogger. I began to use Facebook and Twitter to connect with readers. I sent an email every day requesting a review from established book reviewers. I made my own book trailers using Windows Movie Maker. I blogged anywhere I could. I decided I was going to try everything and I said yes to interview requests. I talked a lot about my journey and sales on my website. Pixel of Ink picked up on a few of my books and everything just sort of took off from there.

Do you do anything that you consider out of the ordinary to make your book a success?

I write in many genres: time travel romance, contemporary romance, romantic suspense and thrillers. I think that has helped me. I am lucky enough to have 4 amazing beta readers to read my books. I now pay for a copy editor and proofreader. I try to release a book every four months.

How have you gone about getting the word out about your books?

Releasing a new book every 3 to 4 months helps. Other than that, I try to say yes to most requests. I do a lot of interviews and I blog at least twice a month on my own website. I advertise on

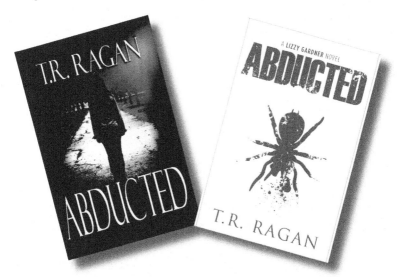

Romance Reviews, Eye on Romance, Frugal EReaders, Digital Book Today and Centsible Ereads. I still make time for writing nearly every day!

What has been your most successful self-published book, and how many have you sold?

Abducted by T.R. Ragan has been my most successful e-book so far, hitting the Top 20 Kindle Paid list twice, reaching as high as #5 in All Kindle E-books. Abducted alone is responsible for half of my overall sales. Abducted has sold 147,000 e-books to date (12 months).

> " Many people have told me that self-publishing is the end to a writers' career, but for me, it's just the beginning.

What are your top tips for new indie authors?

Put yourself out there. Try everything at least once. Experiment with KDP Select, Free Promotions and pricing. Follow your instincts. What works for one author might not work for another. If you don't like to blog, don't do it. Find what works for you. Take your time and enjoy the journey. Be patient.

What do you think about the future of the publishing world?

I see a great future for authors where everyone has more options and choices. Writers will be able to do audio books and foreign translations with the click of a button. Writers will continue to earn high royalties and more and more authors will be able to make a living off of their writing. Brick and mortar stores might be a thing of the past, but people will still be able to buy print books and picture books. The future looks bright to me and it's not about money. It's about opportunities for all. If this self-publishing phenomenon ended tomorrow, I would still be beyond grateful for connecting with so many readers in such a short time.

Any other thoughts you would like to share?

I am excited that writers no longer have to jump insurmountable hoops to get their books in front of readers. I believe there will always be a place for traditional publishers and agents, but readers will be the true gatekeepers, the ones who will decide what they want to read. Writers who self-publish need to put their best work out there. Hire a copy editor and a proofreader. Be patient. Keep writing. Believe in yourself and most importantly believe in your stories because if you don't, who will? Never give up!

Author Websites

http://www.theresaragan.com/

Link to the Author's Amazon Author page

http://www.amazon.com/Theresa-Ragan/e/B004QQBVSO/

Maria Murnane

Introduction

Rom com author Maria Murnane's self-published debut, "Perfect on Paper", was picked up by AmazonEncore (Amazon Publishing's flagship imprint), within a year of release. The book was also a finalist in the chick lit category of the National Indie Excellence Awards and a finalist in the National Best Book Award in the fiction and literature: chick lit/women's lit category. "Perfect on Paper" was followed by "It's a Waverly Life" and "Honey on Your Mind".

The Interview

Tell us about yourself and your background?

I originally had a literary agent for Perfect on Paper, but when she shopped the book to all the major publishing houses, the reply was unanimous - no thanks. After that rejection, which was brutal, my agent gave me the boot. I cried for about three days, then spent about six months rewriting the book. Then I went to a writers' conference and pitched it myself to several more publishing houses, and they all said it sounded great and wanted to read it. So I was so excited again and sent it to all of them. After a few months I finally heard back from all of them - again, thanks but no thanks.

GENRE
Romantic Comedy

So once again I was crushed. Ugh. Then one day my dad (perhaps the nicest man on the planet) sat me down and handed me a book on self-publishing that he had read, along with a little plan he'd written for what I needed to do to publish on my own. He told me he loved my book and that I couldn't let it go, so he was going to help me publish it myself. It nearly made me cry again.

I reluctantly self-published the book, then hit the ground running in an effort to prove the publishing houses wrong. And it worked! Within a year, Perfect on Paper attracted the attention of senior executives at Amazon, who chose it out of more than 10,000 self-published titles for the company's venture into traditional publishing. Since then it has also been published in Hungary and by Random House in Germany, and it's also coming out in Indonesia and Serbia, and it recently reached #2 overall on Amazon. The sequel, It's a Waverly Life, was published by Amazon Publishing in November, and Honey on Your Mind, the third novel in the series, is coming out in July 2012. I've also launched a line of products based on the books that includes witty greeting cards, T-shirts and tote bags at www.honeynote.com.

I've been featured in USA Today, Publishers Weekly, Entrepreneur, Money, Shape, and PopSugar, and I've shared my "never give up on your dream" story with dozens of organizations across the country, including the Harvard Women's Leadership Conference (twice), the Massachusetts Conference for Women, the Baltimore Book Festival, the Texas Conference for Women, the Pennsylvania Conference for Women, and Temple University's Fox School of Business.

Do you do anything that you consider out of the ordinary to make your book a success?

I personally respond to every reader email - apparently a lot of authors don't do this

What are your top tips for new indie authors?

Make sure your book is professionally copy-edited. Indie books can be painful to read because they are often riddled with typos and grammatical errors.

What do you think about the future of the publishing world?

I don't get all the fuss about e-readers, etc. If they get more people reading, then great!

Any other thoughts you would like to share?

If you feel like there is a book inside of you, WRITE IT. No matter who ends up publishing it, there's nothing quite like holding a copy of a book you wrote in your hands.

Author Websites
http://www.mariamurnane.com/

Link to the Author's Amazon Author page
http://www.amazon.com/Maria-Murnane/e/B002BLP3B2/

Russell Blake

Introduction

Author Russell Blake is known for his bestselling thrillers, which include "Fatal Exchange", "The Geronimo Beach", the Assassin Series and The Voynich Cipher, but he has also written the satirical parody "How To Sell A Gazillion e-books In No Time (even if drunk, high or incarcerated)" and the international bestselling "An Angel with Fur: The Story of Lobo the Miracle Dog".

The Interview

Tell us about yourself and your background?

I sold my company and retired relatively young to the Pacific coast of Mexico almost a decade ago, and busied myself with various pastimes, like fishing, boating, loafing. Got bored, wrote as a hobby. Tossed it, as it was crap. Wrote more, tossed that too. Crap, but not as bad. Finally got decent at it, took a run at the trad pub biz, came close, but no cigar. Decided it wasn't for me, so went on to other things.

GENRE *Thriller*

What made you decide to self-publish?

The Kindle. It changed everything. Amazon's elimination of the entire cumbersome hierarchy of agents, trad publishing houses, 18 months latencies on releases, constant rewrites to satisfy corporate imperatives at the expense of artistic, etc. All became moot in 2010, when I first woke up to the Kindle. I watched some of the highly celebrated names succeed - Hocking, Locke, Konrath - and that convinced me that there might be a business there.

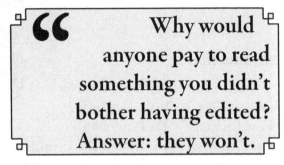

"Why would anyone pay to read something you didn't bother having edited? Answer: they won't.

How long have you been self-publishing?

I published my first book, Fatal Exchange, June, 2011.

What has been the most effective thing that you have done to promote your book?

Building a strong Twitter following, writing a widely-followed blog, and free books on Amazon's KDP Select program. And of course, offering two free books via price matching - Night of the Assassin, and The Delphi Chronicle, Book 1. Night sees 20K downloads a month, and has since it went free Jan, 2012. Delphi goes up and down, and sees around 10K free per month. It's a nice way for readers to sample your work and see if it intrigues them enough to want to buy something.

Do you do anything that you consider out of the ordinary to make your book a success?

I have done several book launches with World Literary Cafe - Melissa Foster's organization - and I believe that has had an effect. In terms of other marketing or promotions, I've only done a few ads, and they were wastes of money as far as I can tell. I think the most unusual thing I have done is to just be myself when tweeting, and not give a rat's ass about political correctness, or "professionalism" or any of that. It's funny to me to see people who have sold 100 books in their life going on about professional this and unprofessional that. Sweetie. Guess what? You have no idea. None. My advice is to just be yourself, and let those who will hate you do so, and those who like you do so.

How have you gone about getting the word out about your book?

World Literary Cafe, Twitter, lackadaisical Facebook (when I remember). Mostly it's been a word of mouth build.

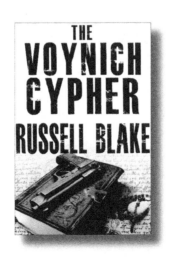

What has been your most successful self-published book, and how many have you sold?

The Voynich Cypher, which I released March 20, has sold over 6K units as of end of April, and seen about 25K+ free downloads. Several of my other titles - King of Swords, Fatal Exchange, The Geronimo Breach - have sold that many, but over many months. Voynich saw a huge surge that has tapered off, but I will be running some promos to see if I can get it back on top.

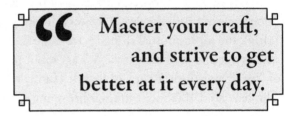

> Master your craft, and strive to get better at it every day.

What are your top tips for new indie authors?

Don't expect to make money. Don't write because you plan to do it for a living. Odds say you won't make it - 99+% don't. Write because you love it, or have a story that needs telling. Once you have written something, treat the publishing part of your life as a business - invest in quality control (editing, covers, proofing), marketing (time on social media), and product development (write more). Writing is one thing. Publishing is a whole different thing. It's a business, and if your business plan is to try to start on a shoestring, throw some unedited junk up on Amazon and hope something sticks, it won't, and you'll fail. This is a very difficult business, and there are hundreds of thousands, or millions, of authors competing with you for the reader's attention. If you put something out that is not absolutely as good as you could make it, meaning professionally edited, with a pro cover, then you are shooting yourself in the head before you even got started. Put another way, why would anyone pay to read something you didn't bother having edited? Answer: they won't. That's the number one mistake I see my peers make. They don't invest in editing and pro covers, and then are devastated when nobody likes their work, or the reviews come pouring in and tear it apart for lack of quality. Completely predictable, but a mistake the majority make. Then again, the majority fail, so there you have it.

What do you think about the future of the publishing world?

I think the trad pub world will need to undergo a paradigm shift, or it will collapse under the weight of its own arcane model. Over the next two to four years, I think it is going to be harder and harder for an indie author like me, who is making a pretty decent living, to want to sign up to being an employee of a publishing house - one expected to work very long hours for a pittance. I look at my reasonable trajectory for 2012 income from self-publishing, and it dwarfs anything I could hope to see if I was trad pubbed, unless I was pushed like I'd just written The Girl With the Dragon Da Vinci Code. I think smart trad pub houses will do hybrid deals with promising indie talents wherein it's more of a partnership, and they can expand a successful, albeit small model, into a mainstream model that has real legs. Either that or they will try to maintain the status quo, charging $12.99 for something I put out for $4.99, and will encounter increasing resistance from the market on making that dog hunt. We're in a time of shift, of change, and in all industries, the groups that innovate, survive. Those that don't are horse and buggy stories.

It remains to be seen how trad pub fares. Indie has its own issues - mainly, a deluge of poor quality garbage hitting shelves. Every author who's written a manuscript in the last 50 years is now dusting it off and uploading it to Amazon, and that isn't good for anyone.

I believe that a year from now, it will be much, much harder for a writer to break and find an audience than it was a year ago, and that trend will continue. But it's also an exciting time, because for some, this is the chance to establish viable indie publishing companies featuring ourselves as the author. Those that are prepared when attention comes, if it ever does, will do far better than those who are trying to hold their fledgling business together with bailing wire and chewing gum.

Any other thoughts you would like to share?

Plan to work very long hours for almost no money, for a long time. Master your craft, and strive to get better at it every day. Apply yourself, and force yourself to write at least an hour a day, every day, with no exceptions. It all starts at the writing. If that isn't compelling and different, than all the marketing savvy in the world isn't going to matter. But once you have a great book, then switch hats, and be a ruthless business person - the book is now a product, and your job is now to polish the product so it is competently executed, then package it professionally, then create a strong value proposition out of your author name over time. You are building a legacy, a brand, that transcends any one title.

Author Websites

http://RussellBlake.com/

Link to the Author's Amazon Author page

http://www.amazon.com/Russell-Blake/e/B005OKCOLE/

Linda Welch

Introduction

Linda Welch's paranormal mysteries, the Whisperings Series, have been hugely popular with readers. Tiff Banks, the white-haired heroine, who talks to "the violently slain", is even a finalist in the Best Hero/Heroine category of the 2012 eFestival of Words Independent E-book Awards! Linda enjoys adding "a splash of humor and dash of romance" to her books and creating unique creatures.

The Interview

Tell us about yourself and your background?

I was born in England and grew up in the countryside, received my education in a tiny village primary school and later at an all-girls secondary school. After leaving school, I worked in the last manually operated telephone exchange in England, and then went into office work. I met a dashing young USAF sergeant in 1971, we married in 1972 and he whisked me off to the USA. We have been married 40 years, have two sons and four grandchildren and now live in the Wasatch Mountains of Northern Utah. I worked for a non-profit child abuse prevention agency for 22 years.

I spent most of my life daydreaming, not

GENRE
Paranormal Mystery

realizing I was actually writing stories in my mind. I began to write them down in the 1980s, as a hobby. That I could publish didn't occur to me. I didn't attend college or university. I don't have degrees in creative writing or journalism. I was not one of those who started writing the moment they could hold a pen and form words. No, publishing was not for me – until 2008, when I met people who encouraged me to do just that.

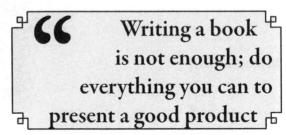

> Writing a book is not enough; do everything you can to present a good product

What made you decide to self-publish?

I became friendly with several traditionally published authors and many aspiring authors who encouraged me to publish, and gave me the inside story on self-publishing versus traditional publishing. There are so many reasons not to publish with a traditional publishing house. Sweating over query letters, wilting at the rejections (if lucky enough to hear back from an agent.) Waiting for up to two years until your book hits brick and mortar bookstores. If the publisher does not make back the advance in a few months, the book is pulled, yet still owned for three to five years by the publisher and the author can do nothing with it. The pitiful royalty rate, compared to rates offered by self-publishing platforms. I could go on at length. Also, unless the publishing house is positive they have a block buster on their hands, they no longer provide top notch editing and the promotional services they once did. Mid-list authors are lucky if they get a good editor and a few weeks of publicity.

Self-publishing was starting to have an impact on online sales, so I decided to give it a try. Funnily enough, a top agent from a top New York City agency contacted me in 2010 and I signed with the agency, more or less to see what happened. I'm glad I did not give up the rights to my digital books, because that deal did not work out. I am now agent-free and happy.

What is the genre of your book?

Genre is a highly debated topic in the self-publishing community. It was fairly straightforward when most books were publisher by traditional publishing houses, but harder to define now that self-publishers are writing what they want to, and not all fit into accepted genres. Many, like me, had and still have difficulty deciding on genre. I couldn't say my books are paranormal/mystery/detective/humor/romance/contemporary novels, so I advertise them as paranormal mystery and they generally appear in the genre sub-category urban fantasy.

How long have you been self-publishing?

I published my first print book in 2008 using the Lulu self-publishing platform. I discovered Amazon Kindle Direct Publishing in 2009, uploaded my book in digital format and haven't looked back since.

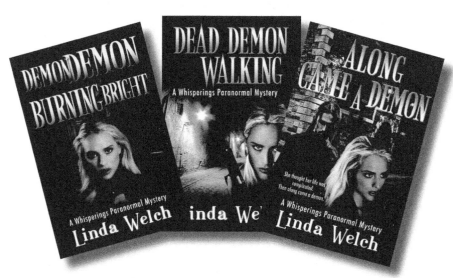

Top Tips from Successful Self-Published Authors

What has been the most effective thing that you have done to promote your book?

The self-publishing world has rapidly become an online community. Online communities are effective for promotion, but many are overloaded with writers trying to sell their books, and readers don't want them constantly shoved down their throats. Therefore, I try to make friends rather than push my books at every opportunity. I get to know readers and other authors and interact on a personal level. If they know you and are interested in what you have to say, they are more likely to read your books and spread the word. I also blog (but not as often as I should) and have sent my books to book bloggers, online review sites and a few for-pay review sites. But I think the majority of my sales come from word of mouth.

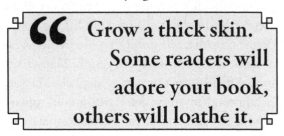

> "Grow a thick skin. Some readers will adore your book, others will loathe it."

Do you do anything that you consider out of the ordinary to make your book a success?

I don't think so. I write paranormal which does not include vampires, werewolves, fairies or any other of the supernatural creatures that are so prevalent nowadays. The "Otherworldy" people in my novels are unique. My books have a strong mystery/detective theme, a little romance and humor. I think readers who are tired of the current overload of supernatural creatures enjoy something a little different.

What has been your most successful self-published book, and how many have you sold?

I didn't start recording sales until January 2010. From January 2010 to April 2012 I've sold 27,000 of the first book in my Whisperings series: Along Came a Demon. I estimate 70% -75% who purchase the book return for the rest of the series, and that makes me happy.

What are your top tips for new indie authors?

Writing a book is not enough; do everything you can to present a good product. Use the services of freelance professional editors, cover creators and formatters. Many reasonably priced professional services are available to help you. Join a writing critique group, and ask for input from beta readers.

Join online reader, writer, and readers/writers communities. They can give you valuable advice, which you should accept graciously. Contact book bloggers and reviewers who review the genre in which you write and offer your book for review.

Grow a thick skin. Some readers will adore your book, others will loathe it; remember, reviews are personal opinions and will differ wildly.

And if an author is serious about becoming traditionally published, he may want to pay attention to a significant trend. Publishing houses are noticing successful self-publishing authors and offering them contracts.

What do you think about the future of the publishing world?

When I came to the States, dishwashers were a common appliance in homes, but not in military housing. Neighbors were buying the stand-alone style you hooked up to a faucet. What would I want with a dishwasher? You had to rinse and scrub the dishes before putting them in, so why not take a few minutes to finish the washing-up manually? And a machine couldn't possibly get dishes clean enough.

Then we moved into military housing with a dishwasher already installed. I would not be without one now.

And microwaves? They couldn't brown a roast or a steak. They were only good for reheating leftovers. And they were so expensive back then. What a waste of money.

Live without a microwave now? No way!

I had similar feelings with the arrival of e-readers. I wanted to hold a book, not a piece of plastic. The text probably wouldn't be as legible as in a print book. What if I dropped it and it broke? Then I looked at the bookshelves in my office, each holding a double row of books with more stacked on top. Over a thousand books I wanted to keep – those I don't keep go to the library used-book sales. And that was just the office. Books dominate the den and bedrooms, too. I did not have space for more books.

We have three e-readers in our house now. I actually enjoy reading from them more than from a print book.

Some of us embrace new technology. Some don't want to let go of what already works for us. But progress happens. It can't be held back.

There is a lot of chatter about digital books killing the print book, especially now one in six Americans own an e-reader, and the number will increase as we become more comfortable with the technology. Kids grow up using screens nowadays, they prefer it that way and so will their children. I see the day when students carry e-readers instead of toting backpacks weighed down by heavy text books, and readers will access their library and borrow books online. Print books won't disappear any time soon, but digital formats will eventually dominate the market.

No matter how we read, we will continue to read, and when I think of the future of publishing, I see publishing houses both large and small adapting to e-book production.

When demand for digital outpaces demand for print, publishing houses will switch their focus. When they no longer need thousands of square feet of space and a huge staff, they will downsize. With no gigantic overhead for offices, office staff, editors, etc., this will also save them financially. Self-publishers already have an impact on publishing and will continue to do so. In April, Jeff Bezos announced that more than 1,000 authors self-publish on Amazon's KDP platform. Many of them publish multiple titles in digital and print formats on multiple self-publishing platforms. This adds up to a lot of self-published books available to readers. Authors who have been rejected by agents and traditional publishing houses have turned to self-publishing. Others don't even consider marketing their book to an agent and take the direct route. Traditionally published authors are self-publishing their back lists and books rejected by their publishers, and making more money than if they sold the same number of print books in brick and mortar bookstores. Whatever the reason they publish, readers are snapping up their books and the lines between traditionally published and self-published are dissolving, at least in the eyes of readers.

Major e-tailers would sell a lot less titles without those by self-publishers.

When the big publishing houses were the gatekeepers, they dictated what we read and did not read, but they are no longer the gatekeepers. With the popularity of online bookstores and readers ability to leave reviews, readers dictate which books are hits and which fall to the bottom of the pile. They are now the gatekeepers. You may think readers, by their reading preference, have always had that power, but they did not when their reading material was restricted to books only the big publishing houses chose for them. Indeed, readers who discover great self-published novels realize their reading experience has actually been stunted by publishing houses that rejected the novels they are now enjoying. Will the future see literary agents and Big Publisher taking note of reading trends for books and genres other than those they publish, and altering their practices in favor of what readers want today? With the relatively lower cost of digital publishing, publishers could put more books on the market, not just the few they believe will make them millions.

I think if traditional publishing houses want to thrive, they must remember success depends on consumer satisfaction. Consumers are readers, clients are authors, and both now have other options. With the wealth of literature out there thanks to self-publishers, readers happily go for reasonably priced books that catch their eye; they don't check to see who published the book, or care. And Big Publishing's clients, the authors, are beginning to realize how much they relinquish in the areas of creativity, control and revenue when they sign with Big Publisher.

What do I think of the future of the publishing world?

Some developments are obvious. Others, I hope to see. I know E-books are the future. I think self-publishing authors and Indie presses will have a bigger presence, and Big Publisher won't be quite as big.

Author Websites

http://lindadwelch.com/

Link to the Author's Amazon Author page

http://www.amazon.com/Linda-Welch/e/B00287TEEG/

Debra Holland

Introduction

Psychotherapist Debra Holland has published both non-fiction and fiction books, but it's her Historical Western Romance Series, The Montana Sky Series, which has captivated readers, won awards and made it on to the USA Today Bestsellers List.

The Interview

Tell us about yourself and your background?

I'm a psychotherapist, corporate crisis/grief counselor, and martial artist. I started writing about twelve years ago after I'd spent several years recovering from earning my Ph.D. Wild Montana Sky is my first book. It won the Romance Writers of America award in 2001, and I thought a publishing contract was right around the corner. I went on to write the next in the series, Starry Montana Sky, as well as some fantasy and science fiction novels.

What made you decide to self-publish?

Despite the efforts of two agents, my novels didn't sell. They languished on my computer, and I turned to writing non-fiction. In the Fall of 2010, agent #3 and a publishing contract

GENRE *Romance*

to write The Essential Guide to Grief and Grieving dropped in my lap. I couldn't even feel excited because I had a five-month deadline.

While I was writing the grief book, a friend emailed me about the success she was having with her self-published books. Like me, she could never sell to New York, although her books are great. She said she was earning $3000 a month from her books. When I read that, I said, "I WANT TO MAKE $3000 A MONTH FROM MY BOOKS!"

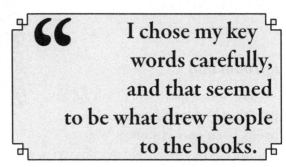

> I chose my key words carefully, and that seemed to be what drew people to the books.

I promised myself I'd self-publish the books as soon as I turned in my grief book. In the meantime, a couple more (unpublished) friends self-published their studies and shared their successful numbers with me. A few days after I finished the grief book, I started another read-through of Wild Montana Sky and Starry Montana Sky, found someone to format the books, and put them on Amazon, Barnes & Noble, and Smashwords.

As soon as I had time to do read-throughs of the first two books in my fantasy romance series, The Gods' Dream Trilogy, I self-published them. Sower of Dreams went up in July and Reaper of Dreams in August. The last book, Twinborne Trilogy: Lywin's Quest, I published in December. So I was able to self-publish five previously written novels in nine months. Little did I know when I read my friend's email, and made a strong wish, that a few months after self-publishing I started earning far more than $3000 a month!

How long have you been self-publishing?

Since April 29, 2011.

What has been the most effective thing that you have done to promote your book?

I wrote the next one. When I self-published book #3, Stormy Montana Sky, I not only had good sales on that book immediately, but the sales of the other two books in the series also popped up.

Otherwise, I've done very little promotion, aside from a few personal and guest blogs. From reports of other self-published authors, most promotion doesn't make much of a difference. Therefore your time is best spent writing your book.

Do you do anything that you consider out of the ordinary to make your book a success?

Nope! I've sort of sat back in astonishment that the books took off.

How have you gone about getting the word out about your book?

I haven't. But I chose my key words carefully, and that seems to be what drew people to the books. There was a whole readership looking for historical Western romance because traditional publishers stopped publishing it. Also, a lot of readers like the traditional (meaning not sexy) nature of the stories.

What has been your most successful self-published book, and how many have you sold?

In one year, Wild Montana Sky has sold about 62,000 and made the USA Today Bestsellers List.

What are your top tips for new indie authors?

Don't rush into self-publishing. Newbie authors don't know what they don't know. Learn the craft of writing. Study self-publishing blogs and books to see if you're a good fit for self-publishing. Make sure you have a professional editor(s) go over the book both for content revisions and for copy-editing.

What do you think about the future of the publishing world?

I think it's SO exciting! Who knows what the future will bring. However, I'm trying to enjoy my success. I'm incredibly grateful to all my readers!

I'm careful how I'm using my royalty income because if it all went away tomorrow (not that I think it will) I want to be in a stronger financial position than when I started.

Any other thoughts you would like to share?

If you don't focus so much on promotion, then you have the time to enjoy writing. Self-publishing has revved up my creativity. I have lots of stories in my head hammering to get out. I also have readers requesting those stories so I always have internal pressure to write. (Not that I do nearly as much as I should.) It's like being in school and always knowing you should be studying or writing papers.

You never know when your lucky break will come. I've seen lucky things happen to a LOT of self-published authors, so keep a positive attitude. Remember to have fun!

Once you publish your book, it's important to have patience. Not all people have the amazing success that I have had with my Montana Sky series. The sales of my fantasies are far more normal (2-10 books a day.) But your books could be published for a long, long time. Small sales build up over time.

Author Websites

http://drdebraholland.com/

Link to the Author's Amazon Author page

http://www.amazon.com/Debra-Holland/e/B004XXKZH8/

J. Thorn

Introduction

Musician and horror author J. Thorn's books include the post-apocalyptic "The Seventh Seal", the Burden of Conquest Trilogy and the "Preta's Realm", all Amazon bestsellers. Thorn enjoys creating "mystic worlds for eyes and ears".

The Interview

Tell us about yourself and your background?

I've been writing all of my life, mostly journalistic and technical pieces. I didn't get serious about writing novels until 2009. I'm a huge fan of epic fantasy, but I never found one that was exactly what I wanted. So I decided to write my own, which eventually became the Burden of Conquest series. Since the summer of 2009 I have written several novels and I seem to have found my voice in the psychological/horror genre. In addition to writing, I am the lead singer and guitarist in an original band called Threefold Law. I write most of the lyrics for our songs so it's no surprise that others have commented on the lyrical quality of my prose. There are a lot of parallels between writing stories on paper and writing them for the stage. I've learned so much about one from the other.

GENRE
Horror / Fantasy

What made you decide to self-publish?

I began to squirrel away manuscripts at the same time I started querying agents. I knew to expect rejection, but I was not prepared for a total lack of response. Not only did I not receive form letter rejections, but in most cases, I never even got an automated email reply indicating that the agent received the query in the first place. Shortly thereafter, Amazon rolled out Kindle Direct Publishing and I started wondering what an agent could do for me that I couldn't do on my own. If I was going to have to promote and sell my book anyways (which you must do even if your agent gets you a deal with a Big Six publishing house), why not keep 70% of the royalties by selling directly to readers? If I were a literary agent, I'd be looking into second career options right now and if the Big Six publishers don't give up their collusion and control of inflated e-book prices, they'll become as irrelevant as the major record labels in the music industry.

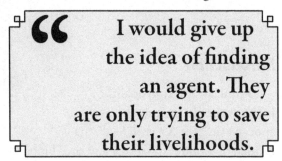

> I would give up the idea of finding an agent. They are only trying to save their livelihoods.

How long have you been self-publishing?

I published on Amazon in the summer of 2011, but I've only been marketing my work since early 2012. The "write a good novel and the masses will buy it" perception is false. You can have a stunning manuscript, but if you do not promote it effectively, you'll be lucky to sell two copies per month.

What has been the most effective thing that you have done to promote your book?

The most effective strategy is to cross-promote with other authors. This does not come naturally to me as I enjoy the solitary experience of writing. However, the new digital marketplace thrives on word-of-mouth and recommendation list driven sales and the best way to utilize that is to align with others trying to accomplish the same thing. I joined The Indie Book Collective in February of 2012 and the sales of my books have been exponential ever since.

Do you do anything that you consider out of the ordinary to make your book a success?

I write fantasy and horror novels as do many other authors. But I also play in a heavy rock band and I think that is out of the ordinary. I can use my writing and my music to cross-pollinate a fan base, a technique that might not be available to other authors and musicians. I also have begun to dabble in the mobile app world as I try to determine what role these devices will play in the future of entertainment.

How have you gone about getting the word out about your book?

Social media is my primary tool in building a brand, but it does not sell books directly. Social media reinforces the meta

message that I am a proven, stable commodity. The idea is to let readers know that I am in this for the long haul and that they can count on more quality product. If you have only one published book, it is an uphill climb to build brand stability. Although not all writers have this luxury, I almost think it is best not to populate your Amazon author page with books until you have at least two or three ready to publish.

What has been your most successful self-published book, and how many have you sold?

The Seventh Seal is the book that launched my writing career. It's not the book I would have chosen to become my marquee title, but those decisions are not for authors to make. Once the book is published, it no longer belongs to you. The post-apocalyptic genre is very hot right now and when I gave this book away for free in conjunction with an Indie Book Collective promotion, I hit the perfect storm. During the five day promotion, The Seventh Seal was downloaded tens of thousands of times. While those free downloads did not result in royalties and did not directly transfer into the paid rankings on Amazon, it vaulted my novel into the matrix of recommendation queues that has kept the book selling consistently. In addition, the exposure from The Seventh Seal lifted sales on all of my other titles. Preta's Realm, for example, sat around 125,000 on the overall paid ranking on Amazon and now it's been consistently in the top 10,000 and remains in the top 40 paid list in the horror/dark fantasy genre.

What are your top tips for new indie authors?

Keep writing. I believe it will be very hard for an independent author to have success with only one or two titles. In this viral, digital world, it still takes time to build a platform and that takes a steady flow of new material. I would also recommend joining groups or collectives like the Indie Book Collective where you can be part of a focused group that is aiming to better all of its members through cross-promotion and teamwork. Finally, I would give up the idea of finding an agent, selling your book to a publisher, and using your book advance to purchase a private island in the Pacific. You don't need an agent or a traditional publisher to be successful and make money as an author, no matter what those in that industry tell you. They are only trying to save their livelihoods and most of us see right through that.

What do you think about the future of the publishing world?

Although it's always dangerous to prognosticate when it comes to technology, I think we're seeing that future right now. Readers will not care if a book has been published by a corporation or the author. They will want well-written, affordable books that can be instantly read on an electronic device. Paper will become a niche market and retail brick and mortar book stores will disappear completely very soon. Much of this is already happening.

Any other thoughts you would like to share?

There is nothing more satisfying than sharing your creativity with others. Whether it's with a computer, a guitar, a paintbrush, or a scrapbook--let it shine. There is no such thing as creative and non-creative types, only people who choose not to express their creativity.

Author Websites

http://jthorn.net/
http://www.threefoldlaw.com/

Link to the Author's Amazon Author page

http://www.amazon.com/J.-Thorn/e/B004ZVF3MK/

James Somers

Introduction

Pastor James Somers' self-published works include Bible studies and Christian fantasy novels, including The Serpent Kings Saga and The Realm Shift Trilogy. His novels are all about "blending cutting edge with Biblical truth" and they have obviously resonated with readers.

The Interview

Tell us about yourself and your background.

I am forty years old, married and have five sons. I work as a Pastor and a Surgical Technologist in addition to writing.

What made you decide to self-publish?

I began with the traditional route of submitting query letters and printing out manuscripts to send to agents and publishers, and received the customary stack of rejection notices. While in this process, I made the acquaintance of another self-published author who was starting up his own independent publisher. He'd been successful with his first novel and asked me if I would be interested in publishing with his start up. I did and it did better than I expected; all in paperback in 2006 before we'd ever heard of

GENRE
Christian Fantasy

Amazon Kindle and E-readers became all the rage. After he sold his start-up to a larger publisher, I decided that I had no desire to go back to the whole "Big Publishing" process. By this time, e-books were beginning to show some promise and Amazon was allowing authors to self-publish with them through CreateSpace and Kindle.

How long have you been self-publishing?

I've been self-publishing since 2007

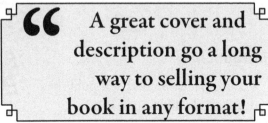

What has been the most effective thing that you have done to promote your book?

Working through Amazon with author endorsements and such, keeping an updated blog, making sure that I have a professional looking product with the best cover I can come up with and networking to do interviews and reviews anywhere I can.

Do you do anything that you consider out of the ordinary to make your book a success?

Out of the ordinary might be the professional product... many self-published novels look like junk on the outside and in the formatting...they don't look appealing and so people rarely get past that. A great cover and description go a long way to selling your book in any format!

How have you gone about getting the word out about your book?

Again, you have to network with other people, do interviews, get reviews from blog sites and other authors... all of these can be useful on your product page at whatever book seller you publish through. Also, I've recently had great success with the Amazon

Select Program…this allows prime members to pick up your novel for free. Free titles appear on bestselling lists on Amazon which others check out. Free promotions on the site are also a useful tool. Give people the first in a series and they are more likely to come back for the rest!

What has been your most successful self-published book, and how many have you sold?

Most of my novels have enjoyed the top spot from time to time and tend to still rotate in that position. I've sold thousands of novels by now. I don't even keep up with the numbers any more. However, The Serpent Kings Saga novels and The Realm Shift Trilogy novels have been some of my top performers recently.

What are your top tips for new indie authors?

Write the best story you can and get the best cover and best synopsis/ description you can for the website where you sell. Get your name around with other authors in your genre as best you can and try to get better known authors to review yours so you can use it on your cover and on your webpage as promotional material.

Top Tips from Successful Self-Published Authors

What do you think about the future of the publishing world?

 I love the direction its headed right now with e-readers and in general allowing authors to seize control of their own work to take it to the public. The Internet and other computer resources have bridged the gap in many ways between what could only be done by a big publisher and what can now be done by the author with minimal help or subcontracting. Higher royalty percentages now belong to self-published authors though the big advances and million sellers still belong to the big dogs. Many of those same big published authors are also beginning to see the differences in the royalties…some are even coming away to the self-published market in order to use their well known names and fan bases to bring greater profits to themselves instead of the publishers. It's the right direction.

Any other thoughts you would like to share?

 I think I've covered it. But remember that its very hard to make a living as a writer and harder as a self-published one. Still, it has its rewards and you may do better than you thought. That's been my finding with my own novels, so far. Above all, write because you enjoy telling the story. When I lose that, I won't write any more.

Author Websites

http://www.jamessomers.blogspot.com/

Link to the Author's Amazon Author page

http://www.amazon.com/James-Somers/e/B002BLLB4K/

Karen Cantwell

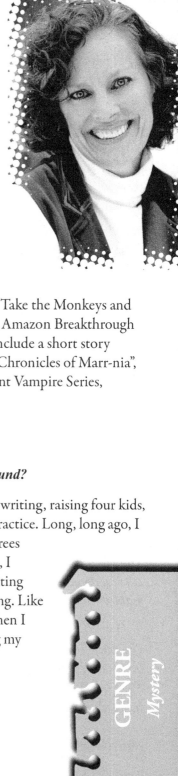

Introduction

Author Karen Cantwell began self-publishing in 2010 and hasn't looked back. Her Barbara Marr comedy mystery series has been a huge hit, with "Take the Monkeys and Run" being a semi-finalist in in the 2009 Amazon Breakthrough Novel Award contest. Her other works include a short story collection featuring Barbara Marr, "The Chronicles of Marr-nia", and "Foxy's Tale", Book 1 of The Reluctant Vampire Series, co-written with L B Gschwandtner.

The Interview

Tell us about yourself and your background?

Currently, I divide my time between writing, raising four kids, and helping run my husband's medical practice. Long, long ago, I graduated from UC San Diego with degrees in Drama and literature. Post graduation, I continued to study various aspects of writing - technical, fiction, poetry, and playwriting. Like many writers I know, I started writing when I was young and always dreamed of having my works published.

GENRE: *Mystery*

What made you decide to self-publish?

For the longest time, self-publishing was never an option in my mind. Early in 2010, however, after receiving one-too-many rejection letters from agents, I grew frustrated. The book I had been querying was the first in a series, and I couldn't seem to get excited about writing a second, when I couldn't even find an agent to attempt to sell the first. I had a vague memory 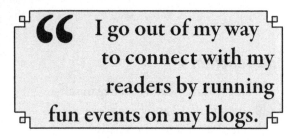 of hearing about a writer who had published her book directly to Kindle, so I began investigating that option since other options had reached dead-ends. At the time, my thought was, "What's the worst that can happen?" Little did I know that not only could nothing bad happen from that decision, but that I was actually embarking on a very exciting and lucrative adventure.

How long have you been self-publishing?

Only 2 years.

What has been the most effective thing that you have done to promote your book?

Write and publish MORE books in the series.

Do you do anything that you consider out of the ordinary to make your book a success?

I don't know if this is considered "out of the ordinary," but I go out of my way to connect with my readers by running fun events on my blogs such as the "Be a character in a Barbara Marr novel Contests" and my "Interview with Barbara Marr." I routinely run giveaways on my website as well as fun reader polls.

I used a reader poll most recently to determine the title of my fifth book in the series. I have received a lot of feedback from readers that they really enjoy the fact that I interact with them. And I have fun doing it, so it's a win-win!

How have you gone about getting the word out about your book?

Initially, when I published that first book, I joined a lot of online forums and discussion groups. Not only did I find readers, but I met other authors who were wonderfully generous in sharing promotion ideas. With time, my readership grew. I have added a feature to my website that allows readers to sign up to receive my blog posts directly to their email. This way, when I have some news (a giveaway or a book release, etc.) it goes on my blog, which in turn goes to their email. I also encourage readers to "Like" my fan page where I post on the same information. I also believe that the interaction I mentioned above helps build word-of-mouth sales.

What has been your most successful self-published book, and how many have you sold?

By actual sales numbers, the first book in the series, by default is the most "successful" since it has been out the longest. I have sold over 60,000 e-book copies of that title. All told, of all books and short stories I have available, I have sold over 90,000 copies - mostly e-books.

What are your top tips for new indie authors?

Approach your venture as a business - once you publish, you are a publisher, not just an author. Be as professional in this business as you would be in any business and provide a professional product. Have your work professionally edited. This is of such vital importance, I can't stress it enough. Take the time and spend the money.

If you're not the most artistic person in the world, have your covers designed by a professional. If you were opening a business in a store-front - a card store for example - you wouldn't paint on some cardboard you found in your garage and call it a sign. You'd hire someone to make an eye-catching, professional sign. Do the same with your cover.

Again, if you're not technically inclined, have your files professionally formatted. You want the reader to enjoy the story and not be distracted by bad writing, editing, and formatting.

Some people have the talent and inclination to be able to do all of these (editing, cover art, formatting) themselves and do it well, but it is my experience that those people are far and few between. Most writers, to put out a quality book, will have to hire a professional in at least one or more of these areas. I hire in all areas, and it always pays off.

What do you think about the future of the publishing world?

More and more authors are going to see the value of publishing their art themselves - they will enjoy the challenge, the never-before-heard-of control they can have over their own work, and the larger income. Major publishing houses will dwindle in size and support mostly celebrities and top-selling authors who have grown so popular that they will need the kind of support a publishing house can provide. More businesses will form and grow that support the self-employed authors - these businesses will provide the professional services of editing, cover art, formatting, and consulting.

Any other thoughts you would like to share?

Since first tasting success in 2010 with publishing on my own, I have been extremely excited about the future for authors. It used to be that writers had to "dream" that some divine, all-knowing individual would grant them the privilege of reaching a reader with our work. In return for that generosity, the writer (artist) had to give up control and rights to the work they struggled over for so long. For most, the money was menial and infrequent. That isn't the case now - writers have options they didn't have before and now they can reach readers without the middle-man. Freedom. It's always a good thing.

Author Websites

http://www.karencantwell.com/

Link to the Author's Amazon Author page

http://www.amazon.com/Karen-Cantwell/e/B003VKZTZM/

Tracey Garvis Graves

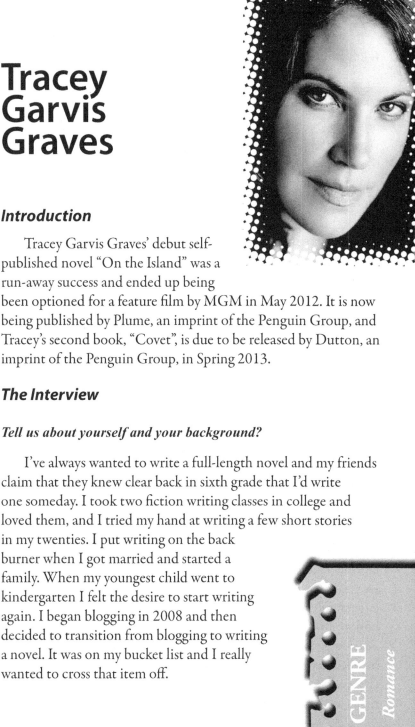

Introduction

Tracey Garvis Graves' debut self-published novel "On the Island" was a run-away success and ended up being been optioned for a feature film by MGM in May 2012. It is now being published by Plume, an imprint of the Penguin Group, and Tracey's second book, "Covet", is due to be released by Dutton, an imprint of the Penguin Group, in Spring 2013.

The Interview

Tell us about yourself and your background?

I've always wanted to write a full-length novel and my friends claim that they knew clear back in sixth grade that I'd write one someday. I took two fiction writing classes in college and loved them, and I tried my hand at writing a few short stories in my twenties. I put writing on the back burner when I got married and started a family. When my youngest child went to kindergarten I felt the desire to start writing again. I began blogging in 2008 and then decided to transition from blogging to writing a novel. It was on my bucket list and I really wanted to cross that item off.

GENRE *Romance*

What made you decide to self-publish?

I queried agents and received nothing but form rejections. I felt like my query letter was strong, but I knew my novel didn't fit neatly into a single genre and the storyline was a bit risky. I was heartbroken, because the people who had actually read On the Island (critique partner, betas, those who received ARCs) really loved it. Once I made the decision to self-publish, I hired a developmental and copy-editor, digital and print formatters, and selected my cover image. It took about three months to complete everything and get to the point where I felt comfortable releasing On the Island.

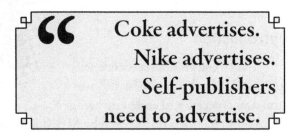

How long have you been self-publishing?

Since September 3, 2011.

What has been the most effective thing that you have done to promote your book?

I don't know if I can pinpoint one single thing, but getting the book in front of readers was so important. I purchased paid sponsorships on Pixel of Ink, Kindle Nation Daily, The Frugal eReader, and Ereader News Today. Some of those websites have Facebook pages with over 200,000+ " likes" which meant that a large number of people would see the book. Visibility is so very important because there are a lot of e-books out there. Coke advertises. Nike advertises. Self-publishers need to advertise. If people see your book and like the cover and blurb, there's a good chance they'll buy it, especially if the reviews are positive. But first they have to know it exists.

Do you do anything that you consider out of the ordinary to make your book a success?

I don't think so. It sounds trite, but you really have to write an interesting story that makes readers want to turn the pages. The desert island premise isn't new, but the people that write to me all say the same thing: they couldn't put the book down because they just had to know what would happen to the characters.

How have you gone about getting the word out about your book?

In addition to the paid advertising, I think the biggest thing that contributed to On the Island selling well is that it appealed to a large demographic and it received a huge push from word-of-mouth marketing. I received quite a few messages from readers letting me know that the book was being discussed on message boards, in reader groups, on Twitter and Facebook, and by book bloggers. Those were things that were technically out of my control, but they're so very important. Reader recommendations can make or break any book.

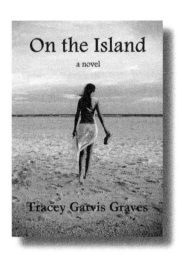

What has been your most successful self-published book, and how many have you sold?

On the Island is my debut novel and the only book I've self-published. I've sold 200,434 copies, across all sales channels, as of May 5, 2012.

What are your top tips for new indie authors?

Choose a good cover, write an effective blurb, and have your book professionally edited and proofread. Make sure your formatting is perfect. Self-publishing is a business and you'll need to spend some money

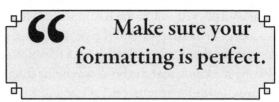

to get started. I know of very few small businesses with such a potentially high return on investment that can be started for under $1,500. Also, don't spam people with requests to buy your book and don't enter the fray when it comes to debates regarding self-published versus traditionally-published books. There's room for all books, regardless of how they arrived in the marketplace, and there are pros and cons for each publishing method.

What do you think about the future of the publishing world?

It's rapidly changing and readers are the people we need to please. Most of them don't notice (or care) who published the book, but if they connect with the story they'll tell others. They are the customer, and they're the game-changers in the future of publishing.

Any other thoughts you would like to share?

Be kind. If someone writes to you and says they loved your book, thank them. There are over a million books on Amazon and if someone downloads yours, be appreciative. Also, don't lash out at people who leave negative reviews because it's incredibly unprofessional. One last thing: you'll need to develop a very thick skin if you want to be in this business.

Author Websites

http://www.traceygarvisgraves.com/
http://www.facebook.com/#!/pages/Tracey-Garvis-Graves/216651501730405

Link to the Author's Amazon Author page

http://www.amazon.com/Tracey-Garvis-Graves/e/B005LDUVJG/

Elena Greene

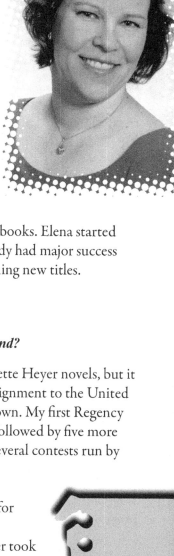

Introduction

Historical romance novelist Elena Greene has won many awards for her Regency romances, inspired by her life-long love of Georgette Heyer's books. Elena started self-publishing just this year, but has already had major success through reissuing her backlist and publishing new titles.

The Interview

Tell us about yourself and your background?

I grew up reading my mother's Georgette Heyer novels, but it wasn't until I went on an international assignment to the United Kingdom that I felt inspired to write my own. My first Regency romance was published in 2000 and was followed by five more Regencies and a novella. My books won several contests run by chapters of Romance Writers of America and my Super Regency, Lady Dearing's Masquerade, won RT Book Club's award for Best Regency Romance of 2005.

I was growing as a writer, but my career took a turn when New American Library ended the Signet traditional Regency line. After a struggle with my muse over what to work on next, I began work on a longer Regency-set historical romance featuring a Waterloo veteran turned

GENRE *Romance*

balloonist. However, my career reached another hurdle when my husband suffered a severe, disabling stroke. For several years, I was too busy caring for him and our two school-aged children to write.

Happily, I am once again finding time to indulge my love of writing and my fascination with the Regency period. Recently, I have self-published my backlist books, along with one new novella. I am reconnecting with readers and have gotten back to work on my balloonist story.

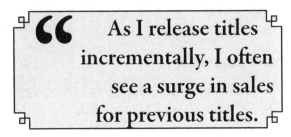

> As I release titles incrementally, I often see a surge in sales for previous titles.

What made you decide to self-publish?

Many of my friends who also wrote Regency romance were doing very well reissuing their backlist books as e-books. This all started happening about when I started to have more time for writing. I hoped that reissuing my backlist would bring in some income and help me re-establish my name.

How long have you been self-publishing?

I have been self-publishing for about seven months.

What has been the most effective thing that you have done to promote your book?

Due to time constraints, I've chosen to prioritize writing new work over promotion. I believe my books have sold well in part because most of them are reissues and have garnered awards and positive reviews. Of the promotion I have done, it is difficult to say what has been most effective. One thing I can say is that as I released titles incrementally, I often saw a surge in sales for previous titles. The books seem to be selling each other, which leads me to suspect that multiple titles improve an author's "discoverability". This in turn makes me feel justified in spending most of my available time writing new work.

Do you do anything that you consider out of the ordinary to make your book a success?

I am not sure this is out of the ordinary, but I do focus on the craft of writing. Since I write historical romance, I do extensive research to make the setting come alive. I also work with a very talented set of critique partners whose advice I take very seriously. Each story is the result of multiple drafts and careful editing. I believe that when writing popular fiction, good storytelling is everything. Writing what I enjoy is important, too. If I don't enjoy it, I doubt my fans would.

How have you gone about getting the word out about your book?

I participate in a group blog, The Risky Regencies, where I post once a week and run the occasional giveaway. Our visitors are avid readers of historical romance, including that set in the Regency era. I also spread the word through the Regency Reader,

Top Tips from Successful Self-Published Authors

a monthly newsletter put out by the Beau Monde, Romance Writers of America's special interest chapter for authors of this genre. I have sought out relevant threads in Amazon's "Meet the Author" forums and posted there occasionally. I have a modest Facebook page and have announced my books on several targeted Facebook groups. I ran some Facebook ads at one point but the results are inconclusive. I couldn't correlate the ads with an increase in sales, although they may have helped increase my overall visibility.

What has been your most successful self-published book, and how many have you sold?

Lady Dearing's Masquerade. As of May 2012, I have sold over 30,000 copies of this book.

What are your top tips for new indie authors?

Make sure your book is as professional, inside and out, as those from traditional publishers. Make sure you have written it to the best of your ability, that it is properly edited and has cover that is not only attractive but also suits the contents. Make sure the metadata (the descriptions, tags and search information) in the online catalogs is as accurate as possible, to help readers find and choose your book. If you have multiple books, make sure to include links and excerpts so the books can cross-promote each other. Tune your promotional efforts to your target audience, especially if you write in a niche genre. Be patient with sales; sometimes they grow over time. And keep writing!

What do you think about the future of the publishing world?

This is hard to say. Obviously, e-books will continue to grow in popularity and the roles of traditional publisher and agents will continue to change. Readers aren't interested in searching through a virtual "slush pile" of offerings. Perhaps traditional publishers will find ways to reassert their original role as the tastemakers. Other tastemakers (perhaps online reviewers and bloggers) may continue to increase in importance at the same time.

The best thing about the current surge in self-publishing is that good manuscripts that don't fit easily into traditional publishing lines aren't condemned to moulder in drawers. This provides a greater variety for readers and more creative freedom for writers. But discoverability is important and I have no doubt that will continue.

Any other thoughts you would like to share:

I don't know if the climate will continue to be as favorable for self-publishing as it is now. I do have faith that good stories will continue to attract readers. My own strategy is to remain flexible about changes in the industry but more importantly, to focus on the things over which I have some control: the quality of my stories and my joy in the process of writing.

Author Websites

http://www.elenagreene.com/

Link to the Author's Amazon Author page

http://www.amazon.com/Elena-Greene/e/B001HMPKY6/

Now you've finished the book...

Thank you for taking the time to read this book. We hope that you have enjoyed the interviews with all of the incredible authors. More than that, we hope that you've seen some ways to improve your own writing and self-publishing career.

We wish you an amazing success with all of the writing that you do.

Claire and Tim Ridgway

Before you go...

- if you enjoyed this book, please review it on Amazon/Goodreads/Kobo etc. - it makes a huge difference on whether others will buy it.
- if any of the authors interviewed seemed interesting to you, please buy one of their books ... they will appreciate it!
- let us know about your own writing and success - you can email us on **info@InterviewsWithIndieAuthors.com**

Please visit our website for up-to-date news about self-publishing, top indie authors and the world of writing...

http://www.InterviewsWithIndieAuthors.com

Don't forget to visit the website and get the latest news on indie-publishing...

www.InterviewsWithIndieAuthors.com

Thank you so much!

Made in the USA
Monee, IL
22 September 2021